# FREDERICK DOUGLASS
# ON WOMEN'S RIGHTS

PHILIP S. FONER, EDITOR

# FREDERICK DOUGLASS ON WOMEN'S RIGHTS

DA CAPO PRESS • NEW YORK

Library of Congress Cataloging in Publication Data

Douglass, Frederick, 1817?-1895.
    Frederick Douglass on women's rights / Philip S. Foner, editor.—1st Da Capo
Press ed.
        p.    cm.
    Includes index.
    ISBN 0-306-80489-1
    1. Women's rights—United States. I. Foner, Philip Sheldon, 1910.    . II. Title.
HQ1236.5.U6D68   1992                                                    92-17609
323.3′4—dc20                                                                CIP

First Da Capo Press edition 1992

This Da Capo Press paperback edition of *Frederick Douglass on Women's Rights*
is an unabridged republication of the edition published in New York in Westport,
Connecticut in 1976. It is reprinted by arrangement with Greenwood Press.

Published by Da Capo Press, Inc.
A Subsidiary of Plenum Publishing Corporation
233 Spring Street, New York, N.Y. 10013

*No man, however eloquent, can speak for woman as woman can for herself.*

*Nevertheless, I hold that this cause is not altogether and exclusively woman's cause. It is the cause of human brotherhood as well as the cause of human sisterhood, and both must rise and fall together. Woman cannot be elevated without elevating man, and man cannot be depressed without depressing woman also.*

*Frederick Douglass in an undated speech to a Woman Suffrage Convention.*

# CONTENTS

# PREFACE

In their long, continuing struggle for equality, American women have had to rely primarily on their own resources. This is not to say, however, that men have not helped advance their cause. Throughout our history they have had the vigorous support of a group of men who lent their names and voices to the woman's movement in the face of ridicule and even violence. William Lloyd Garrison, Theodore Parker, Wendell Phillips, Thomas Wentworth Higginson, Frederick Douglass, William Henry Channing, Henry Ward Beecher, Charles Lenox Remond, Henry B. Stanton, and Parker Pillsbury were among those active in the early woman's movement. According to woman's own testimony, foremost among them was Frederick Douglass. For when the American women who led the early movement were asked later in their lives to suggest the names of men who should be placed on an honor roll of male supporters, the list was invariably headed by this man who, having been born a slave in Maryland, had known oppression first-hand. "He was the only man I ever saw who understood the degradation of the disfranchisement of women," said Elizabeth Cady Stanton, the pioneer of the American woman's rights movement. On July 25, 1919, the *Atlanta Constitution* reported that in opposing the Georgia legislature's ratification of the Nineteenth Amendment granting woman suffrage, white supremacist representative J. B. Jackson climaxed his argument with the statement: "Frederick Douglass is the father and Susan B. Anthony, who received the Negro in her home, is the mother of this amendment!"

The writings and speeches of Frederick Douglass collected in this volume provide ample explanation of both the choice of names and the racist attack. Since suffrage was the major, though not the sole, concern of the nineteenth-century woman's rights movement, it is not surprising that Douglass frequently dealt with the issue of votes for women. But he also spoke and wrote resolutely on the need for women to reach their full potential by participating in every phase of American society as well as in all the decisions shaping that society. No one was more insistent in pointing out that the oppression of women violated the great principles proclaimed at the birth of the American Republic. He was, in short, as he himself said, in favor of "absolute justice and perfect equality" for women.

Proud of being black, Douglass prided himself equally on being a "woman's rights man." But he was a black "woman's rights man," and he never hesitated to remind the white women who led the movement that, while they continually experienced oppression in a male-dominated society, black women endured an even greater oppression in a *white,* male-dominated society.

There have been numerous collections of the writings and speeches of the women pioneers who supported the woman's cause, but this is the first collection of the writings and speeches of a "woman's rights man." The fact that it presents the point of view of a black "woman's rights man" gives it added significance.

Several of Douglass's speeches on woman's rights were originally published in journals devoted to the movement and are reprinted below. But a number have remained in manuscript form in the Frederick Douglass Papers originally housed in the Frederick Douglass Memorial Home in Anacostia, District of Columbia and recently transferred to the Manuscripts Division of the Library of Congress. These speeches are published here for the first time.   In the preparation of this work, I have had the cooperation of the libraries of Lincoln, Columbia, Cornell, Syracuse, Harvard, and Howard Universities, the New York and Boston Public Libraries, and the Library of Congress. I wish to express my appreciation for the assistance so kindly rendered.

Philip S. Foner

Lincoln University, Pennsylvania
July 1975

# FREDERICK DOUGLASS
# ON WOMEN'S RIGHTS

# INTRODUCTION

On the morning of July 19, 1848, in the village of Seneca Falls, New York, the Wesleyan Chapel was about to become the setting for the first woman's rights convention ever to be held anywhere in the world. Some two hundred persons, including thirty-two men courageous enough to run the risk of being branded "hermaphrodites" and "Aunt Nancy Men," crowded into the chapel. Only one man was to play a prominent part in the proceedings. He was Frederick Douglass.

The women who initiated the world's first organized gathering for woman's rights were veterans of the anti-slavery movement. While making invaluable contributions to the abolitionist movement, they had also earned for their sex the right to speak and participate in public affairs. Having advanced the cause of human freedom along two fronts, they had now taken the step to organize a movement for economic and political rights for women. What caused them to take this step?

On July 14, 1832, *The Liberator*, published in Boston by William Lloyd Garrison, proudly announced the formation of the first Female Anti-Slavery Society at Providence, Rhode Island. It was followed by a society in Salem the next year, and, by 1834, there were at least ten such groups in Massachusetts (including one of black women), two in Maine, one in Connecticut, one in New Hampshire, and societies in New York City, Boston, and Philadelphia. Societies also sprang up in the West, and the first anti-slavery organization in Michigan was a female society organized in Adrian in 1834. By the end of the decade, there were female societies in every state in the North, with the largest number in Massachusetts.

The constitution of the Boston Female Anti-Slavery Society expressed in simple and direct language the sentiment inspiring the women who formed these organizations: "Believing slavery to be a direct violation of God, and productive of a vast amount of misery and crime, and convinced that its abolition can only be effected by an acknowledgement of the justice and necessity of immediate emancipation . . . we hereby agree to form ourselves into a Society."[1] The constitution of the Winthrop (Maine) Female Anti-Slavery Society pointed to the responsibility of white women, as Christians, to their suffering black sisters in bondage. It noted with horror the "intellects wasted, sentiments perverted, feelings outraged, and souls lost through the operation of a system which annuls the marriage tie, destroys all parental and filial obligation, denies the right of the mother to call her slumbering babe her own, produces every species of licentiousness and sets at naught the laws of God and nature."[2]

The societies usually pledged themselves to disseminate the truth about slavery in order to convince the nation of the sin of slaveholding and thereby to bring about immediate emancipation. They also vowed to attempt to dispel prejudice against people of color and to help them secure their civil and economic rights. Finally, in order to weaken the economy of the South, they renounced, insofar as possible, the use of products made by slave labor.

Perhaps their greatest contribution, and certainly the one in which the greatest number of women were able to participate, was in the raising of funds necessary to carry on the anti-slavery work. Money-raising became a combination of social function and anti-slavery education, and in Boston, Philadelphia, and Cincinnati, it developed into a traditional institution of the abolitionist movement in the form of the Annual Anti-Slavery Fair.

The fair was usually held during the week before Christmas to enable friends of the slaves to buy Christmas gifts and at the same time contribute to a cause dear to their consciences. All through the year, female societies and sewing circles of the surrounding area busied themselves sewing articles for the fair. Friendly merchants made donations or sold articles at wholesale to the ladies.

The receipts from the Boston Fair increased annually from $300 in 1834 to $5,270 in 1857, when a subscription list was substituted for the fair. The Philadelphia Society was credited with raising $35,000 during the anti-slavery crusade. Large or small, the funds raised at the fairs were unquestionably, in the words of Garrison, a "source of life-sustaining energy" to the anti-slavery movement, not only financially but educationally as well. As a social function, the fair made many new friends for the slaves, enlisting the interest of men and women who were not prepared to make greater sacrifices.[3]

Another general activity of the female societies was the circulating of petitions. *The Liberator* of January 2, 1836, announced: "Honor to the Ladies! A very large proportion of our paper today is occupied with the report of an animated and important debate in Congress excited by the petitions of ladies for the abolition of slavery in the District of Columbia." This was no exaggeration. Over half of the hundreds of thousands of memorials presented to Congress were signed by women.[4] In 1835, when the petition campaign was only beginning in earnest, the Massachusetts Anti-Slavery office tabulated a District of Columbia petition which was twenty-seven feet long and contained 3,309 male and 4,180 female names.[5] In 1837, Congressman Caleb Cushing from the Essex (Mass.) north district presented 3,924 names from his district, all of which were of women. In a letter to the *North American Review,* he criticized the women for "interfering by petition in the political duties of society." Such preoccupation, he wrote, would cause them to sacrifice "all that delicacy and maternal tenderness which are among the highest charms of woman. Here be the domain of the moral affections, the empire of the heart." Let her, he counseled, "leave the soul-hardening struggles of political power to the harsher spirit of man."[6] The *New York Sun* echoed this advice with an order that women go home to shaking bedticks.[7]

Such criticisms became louder as women continued their anti-slavery activities by speaking in public and performing other such "unladylike" acts in behalf of the slave. The first American-born woman to speak publicly in the United States was Maria W. Stewart, a black resident of Boston. She delivered four lectures in Boston in 1832 and 1833 urging both abolition of slavery and equality for women. The Grimké sisters, Sarah and Angelina, coming from a slaveholding family in South Carolina, made a tremendous contribution to the cause on the lecture platform. The testimony of these aristocratic southern ladies carried great weight with their audiences, for they "spoke as if they were a part of a system—a penitent part."[8] As their audiences grew in size, churches were called upon to decide whether their pulpits should be used to expound the controversial anti-slavery position. The Biblical injunction "Let your women keep silence in the churches" was used to justify opposition to their speaking from the pulpit. The opposition became so intense that the Massachusetts Association of Congregational Ministers sent out a pastoral letter ordaining that "agitating subjects" should not "be forced upon any church as matters for debate at the hazard of alienation and division" and that allowing women to speak "threatened female character with widespread and permanent injury—the vine usurps the role of the elm."[9]

But the Grimké sisters went on lecturing. While pulpits resounded with opposition, Sarah Grimké wrote a series of articles proving that woman's rights were bound up with the cause of human freedom. She boldly asserted that if women surrendered the right "to speak this year, we must surrender the right to petition the next year and the right to write the year after. What then can woman do for the slave when she is herself under the feet of man and shamed into silence?"[10]

But there were many anti-slavery men and women who were against intertwining the cause in the "woman question." Angelina Grimké gave a persuasive argument for linking the two when, speaking in behalf of twenty thousand women signers of an anti-slavery petition, she told the Massachusetts legislature: "American women have to do with slavery not only for moral and religious but political reasons. We are citizens of a Republic, and our honor, happiness, and well-being are bound up in its politics, government and laws."[11] In speaking for the slave, woman could not help but speak for herself.

In 1839, the "woman question" became a pivotal factor in the anti-slavery movement. On May 7, the American Anti-Slavery Society, at its annual convention, voted by 180 to 140 to allow all *persons* to be seated as members. One hundred and twenty members went on record protesting the decision, on the basis that granting women the right to speak, vote, and hold office went counter to the rules of propriety and constituted a breach of faith against those who joined the society believing it to be an organization of men. The protesters also charged that the action would tie the anti-slavery movement to a cause extraneous and foreign to its purpose.

Those in favor of women's participation stated that the constitution of the American Anti-Slavery Society made no distinction between men and women, but merely said that "All persons who consent to the principles" were to be admitted. The Executive Committee published a statement declaring that the convention's action was not to be construed as committing the society to the principle of women's equality with men in public affairs.[12] It soon became evident that there was a serious split in the organization.

By the end of the month, the New England Anti-Slavery Society, too, divided on this subject; a group led by Reverend Amos Phelps left the Massachusetts Anti-Slavery Society and organized the Massachusetts Abolition Society. They announced that the old organization had perverted the movement "to purposes and objects not contemplated in our bond of union, attaching a cause which is a millstone to sink to the depths of a bottomless ocean the hopes of enslaved millions."[13] This was the beginning. One year later, in May 1840, the split in the American Anti-Slavery Society over the "woman question" was complete. After Abby Kelley was elected to the Business Committee by a vote of 557 to 440, the opposition left the convention and organized the American and Foreign Anti-Slavery Society. Two anti-slavery organizations were now in existence. While the "woman question" was only one of a number of issues on which there was growing opposition to Garrison's leadership of the American Anti-Slavery Society (others were his anti-clericalism and his "no-government, no-political action" theories),[14] it was of major significance.

Lydia Maria Child answered the charge that the woman's rights movement was "excess baggage" on the anti-slavery train by stating that it was an inevitable outcome of that struggle. Anyone with a reasonable amount of farsightedness could see that "a struggle for the advancement of any principle of freedom would inevitably tend to advance all free principles," she wrote, "for they are connected like a spiral line, which, if the top be put in motion, revolves even to the lowest point."[15] Here again was proof that, in speaking for the slave, woman could not avoid advancing her own cause.

The final act of the "woman question" in the anti-slavery drama was enacted at the World Anti-Slavery Convention in London that same year—1840. The American women delegates from the anti-slavery societies found themselves voted out of the convention and seated behind a bar and curtain, screening them from the public view. The explanation given was that the admission of women was contrary to English custom and would offend the prejudices of some and shock the religious sentiments of others. But it was there in London that Lucretia Mott and Elizabeth Cady Stanton met and talked of another convention—a convention of American women that would launch the battle to eradicate such discrimination as this which humiliated them so deeply. This dream was not to materialize until 1848, but in that year, these anti-slavery women, together with many others, such as Maria Weston Chapman, Susan B. Anthony, Abby Kelley, and Lucy Stone, and a number of "woman's rights men," met in Seneca Falls, New York, and laid the foundation of the woman's rights movement.

\*      \*      \*      \*

Frederick Douglass was only ten years removed from slavery when he attended the Seneca Falls Convention. He was born in February 1817, somewhere in Tuckahoe, Talbot County, on the eastern shore of Maryland, the son of an unknown white father and Harriet Bailey, a slave. As a child, he suffered much from both a lack of nourishing food and the cold. Regardless of the temperature or the time of year, a slave child was clothed only in a tow-linen shirt which reached the knees and was changed only once a week. Many years later, he still had vivid memories of ugly gashes in his feet caused by frostbite.

Douglass grew to detest slavery. He saw slaves brutally whipped; worked from sunrise to sunset six days a week; fed insufficient amounts of pork or fish and low-quality meal; and sheltered in dirty, crowded, uncomfortable quarters in which the clay floors were their only beds.

Douglass's mother was hired out to a farmer twelve miles away, and whenever possible she would walk the distance after a day of labor in the field, visit briefly with her chlildren in the middle of the night, and then return to the farm to begin another day of labor at dawn. These visits ceased during Douglass's seventh year, when she died. He was not even allowed to attend her funeral.

A major turning point in Douglass's life occurred in 1825, when his mistress, Mrs. Thomas Auld, at his request, began teaching him to read. In a short time, he had mastered the alphabet and was learning to spell words of three and four letters.

At this point, Mrs. Auld informed her husband of her efforts to teach Douglass to read and of her pupil's mental agility. Astounded at his wife's naiveté, Auld ordered her to discontinue the instruction, explaining in Douglass's presence that education would spoil even the best of "niggers" by making them unmanageable, discontented, and determined to run away. The lessons ceased, but Douglass was impressed by Auld's assertion that education and freedom were somehow related. He resolved to learn to read and write despite his master's stern opposition and without Mrs. Auld's aid—indeed, over her objections. To accomplish this purpose, he made the streets of Baltimore, where he now worked as a slave, his school and used his white playmates as teachers. Out of his pocket would come the leaves of books he had raked "from the mud and filth of the gutter," a copy of his Webster's spelling book, and a slice of bread to pay for his lessons.

By the time he was twelve or thirteen, Douglass had learned to read and had turned his attention to writing. While working in the Baltimore shipyards, he watched the carpenters label the prepared pieces of timber with letters indicating the part of the ship for which they were designed, and he practiced drawing these letters in his spare time. Then, using the fences as his copybooks and blackboards, and chalk as his pen and ink, he learned to write.

In the evenings, after a day's work in the shipyards, Douglass extended his education. He met free Negroes who were well versed in literature, geography, and arithmetic, and he sought to learn from them. As a slave, he was not able to join any of the forty benevolent institutions established by the free Negroes of Baltimore, but he was permitted, by special dispensation, to become a member of the East Baltimore Improvement Society. Here, he took a prominent part in debates and here, too, he met Anna Murray, who afterward became his wife. Anna was one of twelve children of slave parents and the first of their five children born in freedom, escaping by one month the fate of her older brothers and sisters born in slavery.

On Monday, September 3, 1838, Douglass bade farewell to slavery. From a black seaman friend who was his height, he borrowed a sailor's suit and a sailor's "protection," a paper listing physical features of its owner who, as a free American sailor, could move about the country. (The suit was later returned to its owner by mail.) In the late afternoon of September 3, Douglass arrived in Philadelphia and then went on to New York City, where he was joined by Anna Murray. On September 15, twelve days after his escape, they were married by the Reverend James W. C. Pennington, who had fled from a Maryland master ten years earlier. Two days later, they were on their way to New Bedford, Massachusetts, where Douglass believed that his skill as a caulker would secure him a livelihood. But white racism prevented him from working at his trade, and for three years Douglass led a hand-to-mouth existence as a day laborer. In 1841, following the discovery that he possessed a talent for the public platform, he became an abolitionist lecturer.[16]

Douglass was indebted to women for his legal freedom. While he was on an anti-slavery tour of England in 1846, a group of British anti-slavery women, led by Ellen and Anna Richardson of Newcastle, raised $711.96 to purchase his emancipation from his master in Maryland.[17] A group of British anti-slavery women also raised funds to enable Douglass to purchase a printing press and establish his own paper, *The North Star*. Julia Griffiths, the daughter of a close friend of William Wilberforce, the British abolitionist, organized the campaign for Douglass's paper and furnished him with a "valuable collection of books, pamphlets, tracts and pictures" to use as editor of the paper he was to found in Rochester, New York, in December 1847.[18]

Douglass chose Rochester as the site of his paper largely because the city boasted an active Female Anti-Slavery Society. The society had been organized in 1835 and with it were associated some of the outstanding women of the country—Elizabeth Cady Stanton, Susan B. Anthony, Amy Post, Sally Holley, Mrs. Samuel D. Porter, and the black anti-slavery advocate, Sojourner Truth. Douglass was convinced that the Female Anti-Slavery Society would help build the circulation and meet the operating expenses of his anti-slavery journal. He was not disappointed, for the society organized fairs for the specific purpose of sustaining *The North Star*. So, too, did black women. In Phladelphia, they organized the North Star Association, "intended especially to aid the *North Star*."[19]

Thus, women played an important role in the founding and continued existence of Douglass's paper. Indeed, were it not for Julia Griffiths, the paper would have been forced to suspend publication on many occasions. When she learned in the spring of 1848 that *The North Star* was in financial trouble, she wound up her affairs in England and came to Rochester with her sister to help put the journal on its feet. "She came to my relief," Douglass wrote later, "when my paper had nearly absorbed my means, and I was heavily in debt, and when I had mortgaged my house to raise money to meet current expenses; and in a single year, by her energetic and effective management, enabled me to extend the circulation of my paper from 2,000 to 4,000 copies." In a single year, too, she paid off a debt of between seven and eight hundred dollars.

With the assistance of the Rochester Ladies' Anti-Slavery society, of which she was secretary, she organized fairs, published gift-books, and conducted numerous other activities on behalf of Douglass's paper. When paying tribute to those who had enabled him to continue as an anti-slavery editor, Douglass noted that "we are indebted to none more than to the ever active and zealous friend of the slave, Miss Julia Griffiths."[20]

In reports from communities he was visiting, Douglass regularly devoted space in his paper to the activities of anti-slavery women, black and white. Of the North Star Association, he wrote: "We anticipate much good to our cause, through the country at large."[21] He constantly stressed the unique contribution of the annual fairs conducted by black and white anti-slavery women, crediting them not only with "attracting attention to the subject of slavery," but with playing an important role in "removing the green-eyed monster— prejudice against color." For the women who organized the fairs, he had only the highest words of praise. Thus he wrote in *The North Star* of January 8, 1848:

> We never feel more ashamed of our humble efforts in the cause of emancipation than when we contrast them with the silent, unobserved and unapplauded efforts of those women through whose constant and persevering endeavors this annual exhibition is given to the American public. Anti-slavery authors and orators may be said to receive compensation for what they do, in the applause which must, sooner or later, redound to them; but not so with the thousands whose works of use and beauty adorn this fair. It is for them to work, unnoticed and unknown, and sometimes unenquired for, and many of them unable to see the good that results from their efforts.

Traveling with Abby Kelley and other anti-slavery women during his early lecture tours, Douglass learned to admire at first hand the courage of these women in defying mobs and insisting on addressing audiences in public, despite threats to their personal safety. He learned much, too, from Charles Lenox Remond, the best known black abolitionist until Douglass appeared on the scene, and from his sister, Sarah P. Remond, who was active in both the abolitionist and woman's rights movements. Remond was one of the very early "woman's rights men," and as a delegate to the World Anti-Slavery Convention in London in 1840, he refused to take his seat because women delegates were excluded. Douglass traveled frequently with Remond on the anti-slavery circuit, and he noted with pleasure how his fellow abolitionist usually included some reference to discrimination against women in his speeches.

It did not take Douglass long to discover that many of the arguments advanced to justify the enslavement and persecution of black people were also employed to uphold male supremacy. The New York *Herald*, a fervent defender of slavery and a bitter opponent of woman's rights, editorialized: "How did woman become subject to man, as she now is all over the world. By her nature, just as the negro is and always will be, to the end of the time, inferior to the white race." Little wonder that Douglass saw early that the Negro's cause and the woman's cause were intertwined and that *The North Star*, from its very first issue, featured the slogan: "Right is of no sex."[22]

While Douglass believed that the anti-slavery movement was doing much "for the elevation and improvement of women," he understood fully the need for an independent, organized movement to achieve equal rights for women. On July 14, 1848, *The North Star* carried this historic announcement:

A Convention to discuss the Social, Civil and Religious Condition and Rights of Women, will be held in the Wesleyan Chapel at Seneca Falls, New York, on Wednesday and Thursday, the 19th and 20th of July instant.

During the first day, the meetings will be exclusively for women, which all are earnestly invited to attend. The public generally are invited to be present the second day, when Lucretia Mott of Philadelphia, and others, both ladies and gentlemen, will address the Convention.

While other papers also carried news of the convention, *The North*

*Star* was one of the very few that did not include editorials hurling ridicule and anathema at the sponsors.

A few days before the convention was scheduled to open, Elizabeth Cady Stanton, the driving force behind the meeting, joined with Lucretia Mott and others to draw up the Seneca Falls Declaration of Sentiments and Resolutions. They used the Declaration of Independence as a model:

> We hold these truths to be self-evident; that all men *and women* are created equal . . .

> The history of mankind is the history of repeated injuries and usurpations on the part of man *toward woman,* having in the direct object the establishment of absolute tyranny over her. To prove this let the facts be submitted to a candid world.

They listed eighteen such facts and at the head of the list placed what they considered the main grievance: "He has never permitted her to exercise her inalienable right to the elective franchise."[23]

With James Mott, Lucretia's husband, in the chair, the Declaration of Sentiments was read to the delegates and adopted unanimously. Eleven other resolutions were also adopted unanimously. They set forth such demands as the right of women to personal and religious freedom; the right to testify in courts; equality in marriage and the right to own their own children; the right to own property and to claim their own wages; and the right to education and equality in trades and professions.

The twelfth resolution did not have such easy adoption. It read: "*Resolved,* That it was the duty of the women of this country to secure to themselves their sacred right to the elective franchise." Even before the convention opened, Elizabeth Cady Stanton had been warned that the proposed resolution on the franchise was too radical a step. Lucretia Mott felt that the demand for the vote was too advanced for the times. "This will make us ridiculous," she cautioned. "We must go slowly."

But Stanton was determined to press the issue, and she looked about the convention for an ally. "I knew Frederick, from personal experience, was just the man for the work," she told an audience of suffragists years later. Hurrying to Douglass's side, Stanton read him the resolution, and, having been reassured that he would take the floor in her support, she determined to hold to her purpose.

When she introduced her daring proposal, the general sentiment appeared to be moving against the resolution, and it seemed that it would go down to defeat. It was at this critical juncture that Douglass asked for the floor and delivered an eloquent plea in behalf of woman's right to the elective franchise. The resolution was then put to a vote and carried by a small margin.[24]

Years later, a tablet was erected commemorating the occasion. It read:

> *On this spot stood the Wesleyan Chapel*
> *Where the first Woman's Rights Convention in the World's*
>     *History was held July 19 and 20, 1848*
> *Elizabeth Cady Stanton moved this resolution*
>     *which was seconded by Frederick Douglass*
> *That it was the duty of the women of this country*
>     *to secure to themselves their sacred right*
>     *to the elective franchise.*

In 1888, a few years before his death, Douglass recalled his role at the Seneca Falls Convention and told the International Council of Women:

> There are few facts in my humble history to which I look back with more satisfaction than to the fact, recorded in the history of the Woman Suffrage movement, that I was sufficiently enlightened at the early day, when only a few years from slavery, to support your resolution for woman suffrage. I have done very little in this world in which to glory, except this one act—and I certainly glory in that. When I ran away from slavery, it was for my people; but when I stood up for the rights of women, self was out of the question, and I found a little nobility in the act.

On the occasion of the sixtieth anniversary of the Seneca Falls Convention in 1908, the black educator Mary Church Terrell extolled this "magnificent representative" of her race:

> The imcomparable, Frederick Douglass did many things of which I as a member of that race which he served so faithfully

and well am proud. But there is nothing he ever did in his long and brilliant career in which I take keener pleasure and greater pride than I do in his ardent advocacy of equal political rights for women and the effective service he rendered the cause of woman suffrage sixty years ago.[25]

In *The North Star* of July 28, 1848, Douglass praised the action taken by the Seneca Falls Convention and announced his support of "the grand movement for attaining the civil, social, political, and religious rights of women." He bade the women engaged in the crusade his "humble Godspeed." Two weeks later, on August 2, he attended a series of meetings in Rochester to ratify the program of the Seneca Falls Convention. Again he was called upon to argue the suffrage resolution, and "in a long, argumentative and eloquent plea," he convinced many delegates who were hesitant about demanding the ballot. Not only was the proposal adopted, but the women of Rochester, persuaded by Douglass's arguments, voted to petition the state legislature to grant them the ballot and dedicated themselves to continuing the appeal year after year until it was granted. Douglass hailed their stand, declaring "that the only true basis of right was the capacity of individuals."[26]

At the anti-slavery meeting held in Boston in 1850, an invitation was extended from the speaker's desk to all who were interested in a plan for a National Woman's Rights Convention to meet in the anteroom. Nine women responded and entered the dark and dingy room. This little meeting resulted in a call, signed by many prominent men and women, for the first National Woman's Rights Convention to meet in Brinley Hall, Worcester, on October 23, 1850.

Douglass was in Massachusetts at this time, organizing opposition to the Fugitive Slave Act of 1850. He read the call for the national convention to consider "the question of Woman's Rights, Duties and Relations" and arranged his schedule so that he could be in Worcester on October 23. The convention was already in session when he entered the hall to be greeted by a burst of applause. Douglass walked swiftly forward to grasp the hands of another former slave who was present as a delegate—the black woman abolitionist and woman's rights advocate Sojourner Truth. Then he sat down alongside William Lloyd Garrison, Wendell Phillips, Stephen S. Foster, and several other men active in the abolitionist crusade.

The convention was well attended with representatives from nine states present. Its motto, "Equality before the law without distinction of sex or color," was evidence of the influence of the black and white abolitionists. The convention voted to petition the legislatures of eight states to grant the ballot to women. A national committee was appointed to achieve this goal as well as to seek the repeal of property laws discriminating against women and to bring about the opening to women of all governmental and professional positions. Douglass was elected a member of this committee.[27]

In England, a detailed article by Harriet Hardy Mill (Mrs. John Stuart Mill) in the *Westminster Review* noted the Worcester convention and endorsed its proceedings. But in America, the newspapers pelted it with abuse. It was "the Men's Convention," and its members "ismizers of the rankest stamp." The headline in the *New York Herald* read: "Awful Combination of Socialism, Abolitionism, and Infidelity." Its account emphasized that radicals of all beliefs and "of all sexes and colors" attended. "Woman's offices," howled the *New York Mirror*, "are those of wife, mother, daughter, sister, friend—Good God can they not be content with these?"[28] "No," Douglass thundered in reply, as he reported to his readers on the great progress achieved at Worcester.

In spite of this cheap ridicule, the woman's movement gained momentum. Douglass continued to lend it his active support. Indeed, few woman's rights conventions were held during the 1850s at which Douglass was not a featured speaker and whose proceedings were not fully reported in his paper. Invariably, the notice would be accompanied by an editorial comment hailing the meeting and expressing the editor's hope that the proceedings "will have a powerful effect upon the public's mind." In 1853, when Douglass was considering changing the name of his paper, he rejected the proposed title, *The Brotherhood*, because it "implied the exclusion of the sisterhood." He called it *Frederick Douglass' Paper*, and underneath the title were the words, "All Rights For All!" In her unpublished study, "The Woman's Rights Movement in New York State, 1848-1854," Helen T. Shea cites Douglass's paper as the friendliest journal in the state to the woman's rights movement and as an indispensable source of information about the movement's activities.

Since copies of *Frederick Douglass' Paper* after mid-1854 are virtually nonexistent, it is difficult to describe in detail its coverage of the woman's rights movement on the eve of the Civil War. But we do know from Douglass's correspondence that he included material about and by "the sisterhood" in his paper and reported the activities of women wherever they were engaged in "asking for equal political rights with men." In late 1855, Susan B. Anthony even asked Gerrit Smith to read Douglass's weekly for regular notices of woman's rights gatherings.[29]

A temperance man himself—he took the pledge from Father Mathew while in Ireland in 1846—Douglass shared the women reformers' anger that the law placed married women at the mercy of drunken husbands, and he encouraged their efforts both to change the law and to stamp out alcoholism. But when women organized themselves into associations and sent delegates to the men's temperance conventions asking for recognition as equals, they encountered stiff opposition, especially from the clergy.

On January 28, 1852, in answer to the call to a mass meeting of all the temperance divisions in New York State, the Daughters of Temperance sent Susan B. Anthony, Mary C. Vaughan, and Lydia Fowler as delegates. They were accepted as delegates, but when Anthony attempted to speak, she was informed that the ladies were there to listen but not to participate. Thereupon, the women left and announced an evening meeting at which all would be welcome. This meeting was well attended, and the women proclaimed their right to act as equals in temperance reform.

Not content with this action, the women met in Rochester in April 1852 and formed the Woman's New York State Temperance Society with Elizabeth Cady Stanton as president, Antoinette L. Brown vice-president, and Susan B. Anthony and Amelia Bloomer secretaries. Douglass covered their activities in his paper and welcomed the formation of the society. But he took issue with the move led by Amelia Bloomer to limit the right to hold office in the society to women. He aligned himself with Stanton and Anthony in opposing this as a violation of "the principle of human equality"—a violation, in short, of men's rights. Douglass felt that by excluding men from office the Woman's Temperance Society would lose supporters in their battle against those in the temperance movement who wished to deny women equal rights. How, he asked, could women effectively contend for equality in the movement when they denied it to men? In June 1853, the society accepted the logic of this position and admitted men to office.[30]

Douglass learned much from the women with whom he associated at the national and state woman's rights conventions. At one time, he had entertained serious doubts about wives being given the right to share equally with their husbands the disposition of property, since "the husband labors hard" while the wife might not be gainfully employed for wages. But his discussions with Ernestine L. Rose, Elizabeth Cady Stanton, Abby Kelley Foster (now married to Stephen S. Foster), Paulina Wright Davis, and other pioneers of the woman's rights movement convinced him that, even though wives were not paid for their domestic labors, their work was as important to the family as that of their husbands. Once convinced, he acted. He wrote the call for the 1853 woman's rights convention in Rochester, New York, which demanded not only that women should be paid equally with men for their work, but also that women, including married women, should have equal rights with men to the ownership and disposition of property.[31] In *Frederick Douglass' Paper* of December 25, 2853, Douglass urged all citizens of New York to sign a petition to the state legislature, drawn up by William H. Channing, calling for passage of a law which would "place Married Women on an equality with Married Men in regard to the holding, and division of real and personal property."

The women with whom he worked in the movement also gave Douglass a clearer understanding of the economic problems facing members of their sex. When he drew up a plan for an American industrial school for blacks to be established in Pennsylvania, he included a provision for an industrial school which included females. He emphasized that "a prominent principle of conduct will be to aid in providing for the female sex, methods and means of enjoying an independent and honorable livelihood."[32]

On one issue, however, Douglass refused to budge. He was critical of woman's rights leaders who addressed audiences from which blacks were barred. His particular target was Lucy Stone. Douglass often praised this abolitionist and veteran fighter for equal rights for women, but he criticized her for not having cancelled a lecture in 1853 at Philadelphia's Music Hall when she discovered that blacks were to be excluded.[33] Later, he was more severe when he learned that she had invited Senator Stephen A. Douglas of Illinois, one of the architects of the infamous Fugitive Slave Act of 1850 and author of the pro-slavery Kansas-Nebraska Act, to join the women who were to meet in Chicago in 1859 to publicize the women's rights cause. Tossing delicacy to the winds, Douglass bluntly accused her of willingness to advance woman's rights on the back of "the defence-less slave woman" who suffered wrongs compared to which the in-justices—and they were indeed injustices—heaped upon other women were in an entirely different class. "Other women suffer certain wrongs," he reminded Lucy Stone and other woman's rights leaders who followed a similar policy, "but the wrongs peculiar to woman out of slavery, great and terrible as they are, are endured as well by the slave woman, who has also to bear the ten thousand wrongs of slavery in addition to the common wrongs of woman."[34]

Lucy Stone had her defenders, but they were all white. Blacks, including those who publicly supported the woman's rights move-ment, agreed with Douglass's position.[35]

As a result of Douglass's criticism of women, both black and white, who agreed to speak to segregated audiences, the woman's rights movement became more sensitive to the issue of prejudice against black Americans. In some instances, it also brought an apology from the women involved and an agreement to make amends. Elizabeth S. Greenfield, the "Black Swan" who astounded the musical world in the United States and Europe during the early 1850s with her amazing contralto voice, was angrily dubbed the "Black Raven" by Douglass after she consented to perform before an audience in New York City from which "colored persons" were excluded. Stung by the criticism, in which a number of other leading blacks joined, Greenfield voiced "regret" that the management of the Metropolitan Hall had "debarred" people of her color, and wrote: "I will with pleasure sing for the benefit of any charity that will elevate the condition of my colored brethren."[36]

Douglass's disputes with some of the woman's rights leaders went beyond the question of their appearance before segregated audi-ences. Women like Elizabeth Cady Stanton, Abby Kelley, and Susan B. Anthony were close to William Lloyd Garrison. When Douglass split with Garrison over the latter's reliance on "moral suasion" as the major route to abolition, as well as over his opposition to anti-slavery political action and over his view that the Constitution was a pro-slavery document, some woman's rights leaders grew cool to the black abolitionist. Several of them seem to have been influenced by their dislike of Julia Griffiths, whom they resented for the influ-ence she exerted on Douglass. Indeed, this relationship became a major public issue in 1853. It began with the following comment by Garrison in *The Liberator:*

> For several years past, he [Douglass] has had one of the worst advisers in his printing-office, whose influence over him has not only caused much unhappiness in his own household, but perniciously biased his own judgment; who, active, futile, mischievous, has never had any sympathy with the American Anti-Slavery Society, but would doubtless rejoice to see it become extinct; and whose sectarianism is manifestly paramount to any regard for the integrity of the anti-slavery movement.[37]

It did not require much insight for readers to discern that the reference was to Julia Griffiths, Douglass's able assistant in his newspaper office. This attack was by no means the first on Griffiths during the controversy (the *National Anti-Slavery Standard* had already referred to her as "a Jezebel whose capacity for making mischief between friends would be difficult to match"),[38] but until that time no one had publicly raised the question of domestic discord in the Douglass household.

Mrs. Anna Murray Douglass immediately sent a short note to Garrison, stating: "It is not true, that the presence of a certain person in the office of Frederick Douglass causes unhappiness in his family." Garrison printed the letter, but commented that it was "evasive in its language, as our charge had reference to the past and not to the present." A little while later, he denied that he had intended to imply any immorality in his charge and expressed regret that he had ever raised the question of relations between Douglass and his wife.[39] But by that time, the damage had already been done.

Douglass was furious with Garrison for the personal character of his attacks. "He has seen fit to invade my household," he wrote bitterly, "despite the sacredness of my home, to break through the just limits of public controversy, and has sought to blast me in the name of my family." He refused to discuss his family relations in the press, claiming that they involved "considerations wholly foreign to the present controversy" and that "a man's wife and children should be spared the mortification involved in a public discussion of matters entirely private."[40]

This distasteful episode split the woman's rights movement. Mrs. Jane Swisshelm, a foremost spokesman for woman's rights, abolition, temperance, and other reforms in Pittsburgh, condemned Garrison, asking: "How can any man, professing to know anything of the common courtesies of life, drag a woman before the public as the enemy of her own husband, and persist in holding her in such a position, despite her own protest?"[41] On the other hand, Susan B. Anthony assured Garrison that he had her full support and demonstrated her anger at Douglass and Griffiths in a letter to the editor of *The Liberator:*

We were all surprised & shocked at the appearance of Anna Douglass' letter in the Liberator. *Anna did not* to my certain knowledge, intend that letter to cover all the *essentials* of the Liberator charge—for she declared to Amy Post, who happened to call there at the time it was concocted by Frederick & Julia; that she would *never* sign a paper that said, Julia had not *made her trouble.* Said she, *Garrison is right*—it is Julia that has made Frederick hate all his old friends—Said she, I don't care anything about her being in the *office*—but I won't have her in my house.[42]

Griffiths had moved into Douglass's house soon after her arrival in this country.

Unquestionably, Mrs. Douglass regretted her husband's split with Garrison. When the family lived in Massachusetts, she had been close to Garrison's followers; she had been active in the local anti-slavery societies and had many friends there. When the family moved to Rochester, she continued to be active in the local anti-slavery societies, but found it more difficult to make friends in the upstate New York community. She must have often regretted the decision to leave New England and the many friends she had made there among the Garrisonians.[43]

Douglass rarely discussed his wife. However, in a letter to a female friend who had asked him to describe his family, he wrote on April 17, 1857:

Suppose I begin with my wife. I am sad to say that she is by no means well—and if I should write down all her complaints there could be no room even to put my name at the bottom, although the world will have it that I am actually at the bottom of it all. She has the face—I was going to use terms scarcely up to the standard of modern elegance—neuraligia ]sic]. She has a great deal to do, but little time to do it in, and withal much to try her patience and all her other very many virtues. You have doubtless in your experience, met with many excellent wives and mothers, who have been in very much the same condition in which my wife is. She has suffered in every member except one. She still seems able to use with great ease and fluency her powers of speech, and by the time I am at home a week or two longer, I shall have pretty fully learned in how many points there is need of improvement in my temper and disposition as a husband and father, the head of a family! Amid all the vicissitudes, however, I am happy to say that my wife gives me an excellent loaf of bread and keeps a neat house, and has moments of marked amiability, of all which good things, I do not fail to take due advantage.[44]

At the time this letter was written, Frederick and Anna Douglass had four children: Frederick, Jr., Charles Remond, Rosetta, and Annie.

The ailments from which Anna Douglass suffered were not uncommon among nineteenth-century women, and some historians have called them psychosomatic. She continued to suffer from rheumatism, which confined her to the indoors until she died in August 1882. "Mother was the post in the center of my house and held us together," Douglass wrote shortly after his wife's death.[45] The tribute to Anna Murray Douglass by her daughter, Rosetta Douglass Sprague, makes it clear that while her father might at times have been less than flattering to his wife, he was sincerely devoted to her and appreciated her many contributions toward his progress from obscurity to fame:

During her wedded life of forty-four years, whether in adversity or prosperity, she was the same faithful ally, guarding as best she could every interest connected with my father, his life-work and the home. Unfortunately an opportunity for a knowledge of books had been denied to her, the lack of which she greatly deplored. Her increasing family and household

duties prevented any great advancement, altho' she was able
to read a little. By contact with people of culture and education,
and they were her real friends, her improvement was marked.
She took a lively interest in every phase of the Anti-Slavery
movement, an interest that father took full pains to foster and
to keep her intelligently informed. I was instructed to read
to her. She was a good listener, making comments on passing events, which were well worth consideration, altho' the
manner of the presentation of them might provoke a smile.
Her value was fully appreciated by my father, and in one of
his letters to Thomas Auld [his former master], he says: "Instead
of finding my companion a burden she is truly a helpmeet."[46]

Douglass did not permit the differences with woman's rights
leaders to interfere with his support for the woman's cause. He had
been the presiding officer at the National Convention of Colored
Freemen at Cleveland in 1848 and warmly endorsed the resolution,
passed unanimously, which affirmed the equality of the sexes and
invited the women present to participate in the proceedings. Two
months later, at Philadelphia, Douglass was one of the organizers
of a convention of blacks and again played a leading role in bringing
about an invitation to women, white as well as black, to attend and
participate. Lucretia Mott decided to accept. She wrote to Elizabeth
Cady Stanton:

> We are now in the midst of a convention of colored people of
> this city. Douglass & Delany—Remond & Garnet are here—
> all taking an active part—and as they include women & *white*
> women too, I can do no less with the interest I feel in the cause
> of the slave, as well as of woman, than be present & take a
> little part—So yesterday, in a pouring rain, Sarah Pugh &
> myself, walked down there & expect to do the same today.[47]

At the Colored National Convention in Rochester in July 1853,
Douglass, chairman of the Committee on Declaration of Sentiments,
wrote to Gerrit Smith: "We had one Lady Delegate—Mrs. Jeffrey
of Geneva—strange to say we had good sense to make no *fuss* about
it."[48]

Douglass was also a member of the executive committee of the

Radical Abolitionists—advocates of political action to end slavery wherever it existed in the United States—when it met in Worcester in 1860 to consider the feasibility of establishing a political party on strictly anti-slavery grounds. The gathering invited women to participate in the proceedings, thus marking the first effort "to organize a political party upon a basis of absolute justice and perfect equality." Douglass, together with Stephen Foster, husband of Abby Kelley Foster, initiated this stand. It was consistent with Douglass's advocacy of "absolute justice and perfect equality" for women.[49]

Although Susan B. Anthony had sided with Garrison in the dispute involving Julia Griffiths, she solicited Douglass's support in her campaign against capital punishment. She circulated a petition for a meeting in Rochester on October 7, 1858, to protest the impending execution of young Ira Stout, who had been convicted of murder, and to urge passage of a law providing for life imprisonment for all who were convicted of capital crimes. Long an opponent of capital punishment, Douglass not only agreed to sign the petition, but, at Anthony's request, prepared a set of resolutions to be adopted by the meeting. When it became evident that the scheduled chairman had been intimidated by threats of mob violence, Anthony asked Douglass to take the chair. He promptly agreed. Douglass's conduct won over even those women who had allied themselves with Anthony in the Douglass-Garrison dispute.

One of them, Lucy N. Colman, wrote to *The Liberator:*

Amidst a shout of "No" from the disturbers, Mr. Douglass took the chair. His manly bearing and noble presence for a moment awed even these terrible rioters, and the organization of the meeting was complete. . . .

Now again commenced the most diabolical yells. Cries of "Put in a white man"—"Down with the nigger"—"Whitewash him"—"Miss Susan"—"Wimmen," &c. &c., issued from all directions.

Seldom have we heard such earnest eloquence as fell from the lips of Mr. Douglass, as he stood before that maddened crowd, and defended the right of Free Speech. Insulted almost beyond parallel, and to one not imbued with the spirit which, forgetful of self, thinks only of humanity's good, beyond endurance, not once did he forget the dignity of his position or the responsibility of the office with which he was invested. Much of this, so happily did he use his rich and powerful voice, was distinctly heard above the terrible noise of the mob. . . .

Our resolutions were now read by Mr. Douglass, but it was impossible to act upon them. The scene at this time beggars description; yells of the most hideous order, groans, hisses, stamping of feet, whistling, language too vile to pen, were the order of the hour. . . . When the riot became dangerous, the mayor came to our platform and requested our president to adjourn the meeting. This was done. Where *then* was the mayor's protection? Mr. Douglass, with his daughter upon his arm and his sons by his side, left the hall, surrounded by a gang of ruffians, heaping all manner of vile sayings upon him, for the simple and only reason that "he wore a skin not colored like their own."[50]

Thus, on the eve of the Civil War Douglass's relations with all in the woman's movement were once again cordial. As we shall see, the situation was to change after the war.

*      *      *      *

During the Civil War, the country was so engrossed in the conflict that the woman's cause receded into the background. Even the leaders of the woman's rights movement abandoned many of their usual activities and devoted their energies instead to the Sanitary Commissions, Women's Loyal Leagues, and other organizations through which women assisted the government in the hour of its greatest peril. Douglass was so involved before Emancipation in advocating his twin policy—"free the slaves and arm the blacks"—to the Lincoln Administration, and then, during the war, in recruiting black soldiers and outlining his views on the nature of postwar society, that he had no time for other issues. Even some of his more fervent causes had to be set aside. For example, in April 1862 the New York legislature repealed the provisions of the 1860 *Act Concerning the Rights of Husband and Wife*, which granted the mother equal guardianship over her children and gave the widow sole control of the property, in case of her husband's death, for the support of her minor children. Douglass, like other "woman's rights men," was too absorbed in the war to voice a protest. Indeed, during the four years of civil conflict Douglass referred to woman's rights only once, and that was in a speech in Boston on January 25, 1865. While calling for Negro suffrage as an essential part of postwar Reconstruction, Douglass affirmed his belief that "women as well as men have the right to vote, and my heart and my voice go with the movement to extend suffrage to women." But he quickly added that woman suffrage rested upon a different basis than that of the Negro's right to the ballot.[51]

The last observation aroused little comment at the time, and Douglass did not press the point. But it was not long before this issue was to create serious friction between many of the men and women who had been associated for years in the anti-slavery and woman's rights movements. In the last issue of Garrison's *Liberator* on December 29, 1865, Elizabeth Cady Stanton remarked with some anger that many of the male abolitionists were beginning to say that "this is the negro's hour" and that while the black man's right to the ballot was being pressed in their circles, "woman's right is ignored everywhere." The women, she wrote, were not going to be pushed aside by either "white or black male citizens" and were already circulating petitions to Congress demanding that it include women in any legislation dealing with suffrage.

At the same time, Stanton wrote to the *National Anti-Slavery Standard*, and this time she was even sharper. She stated that, with the Thirteenth Amendment ending slavery ratified, the black man was now free, and already a move was on foot to grant him the suffrage. The women had been willing to do their utmost for the freedom of the Negro, so long as he was a slave, and had played a key role in getting the Thirteenth Amendment ratified. But now that the Negro was free, "now, as the celestial gate to civil rights is slowly moving on its hinges, it becomes a serious question whether we had better stand aside and see 'Sambo' walk into the kingdom first." Who could be sure, she asked, that if Negro men secured the ballot, they might not become "an added power to hold us at bay? . . . Why should the African prove more just and generous than his Saxon compeers?" And what about the two million black women in the South? What would their freedom mean if they did not obtain civil rights and the right to vote? "In fact," she went on, "it is better to be the slave of an educated white man, than of a degraded, ignorant black one. We who know what absolute power the statute laws of most of the States give man, in all his civil, political and social relations, do demand that in changing the status of the four millions of Africans, the women as well as the men should be secured in all the rights, privileges and immunities of citizens." In short, suffrage for the black man should not be allowed to deprive woman of her rights, and Stanton urged the *Standard* to endorse the women's petition to Congress.

The *National Anti-Slavery Standard* was irritated by Stanton's reference to "degraded, ignorant" black men. While it published the women's petition, it read her a lecture in which it asserted firmly that "this *is* the negro's hour." The ballot for Negro men, it continued, was necessary in order to assure that the freedom achieved in the Thirteenth Amendment would not become a mockery, with the ex-slave again committed "to the vindictive ferocity of the system from which he seems about to escape." It continued:

> Hence, we cannot agree that the enfranchisement of women and the enfranchisement of the blacks stand on the same ground, or are entitled to equal effort at this moment. They certainly are not identified in the popular mind, and Mrs. Stanton must see that while there is a strong party in Congress who can be brought to vote directly or indirectly for putting the ballot in the hands of the blacks, no considerable portion of those votes could be carried now for an amendment to the Constitution which should include women.

> Thirty years of agitation and four years of war have created this costly opportunity. If we let it pass, it passes forever, or at any rate, for a generation. For that reason we have no right, from an anxiety for something beside justice to the negro, to throw away a single chance of securing it for him. Causes have their crises. That of the negro has come; that of the woman's rights movement has not come.[52]

Douglass did not fully endorse this editorial; on the contrary, he again championed the woman's cause. In February 1866, Elizabeth Cady Stanton pointed to his advocacy of woman's rights as proof that "Douglass understands the philosophy of social life and republican institutions."[53] When the American Equal Rights Association was founded in May 1866 with the aim of securing suffrage for black men and all women, Douglass was chosen one of the three vice-presidents.[54] The *New York Herald's* description of the delegates to the association's convention in November 1866, at which Douglass played a prominent role, read:

> All the isms of the age were personated there. Long-haired men, apostles of some inexplicable emotion or sensations; gaunt and hungry looking men, disciples of bran bread and white turnip dietetic philosophy; advocates of liberty and small beer, professors of free love in the platonic sense, agrarians in property and the domestic virtues; infidels, saints, negro-worshippers, sinners and short-haired women. . . . Long geared women in homespun, void of any trade mark, and worn to spite the tariff and imposts; women in Bloomer dress to show their ankles, and their independence; women who hate their husbands and fathers, and hateful women wanting husbands . . . altogether the most long-necked, grim-visaged, dyspeptic, Puritanical, nasal-twanged agglomeration of isms ever assembled in this or any other state.[55]

The avalanche of ridicule which the press heaped upon the association caused some of the male delegates to the convention to withdraw. Douglass stayed throughout the proceedings and made it clear that he would continue to cooperate with the organization and publicize its program. Nevertheless, during the convention, he clashed publicly for the first time with some of the association's women leaders. He was concerned that Elizabeth Cady Stanton and Susan B. Anthony seemed more interested in the woman question than in solving the problems of Reconstruction and that they were beginning to say they would oppose any extension of suffrage to male Negroes if political enfranchisement of their sex was not included. Douglass warned the Equal Rights Association that it was in danger of becoming "*merely* a woman's rights convention" and appealed that the "women must take the negro by the hand." True, the association had been organized to secure the suffrage for women as well as for black men, but the question of the hour was which group should receive priority. To women, the ballot was desirable; to the Negro, it was a matter of life and death. Pointing to the riots taking place against blacks in a number of cities, Douglass declared: "With us disfranchisement means New Orleans, it means Memphis, it means New York mobs."

Douglass also objected to Anthony's praise of James Brooks, who was then championing woman suffrage in Congress. Douglass pointed out that it was simply "the trick of the enemy to assail and endanger the right of black men." Brooks, former editor of the *New York Express*, a viciously anti-Negro, pro-slavery paper, was playing up to the leaders of the woman's rights movement in order to secure their support in opposing Negro suffrage. Douglass warned that if the women did not see through these devices of the former slave owners and their allies, "there would be trouble in our family." Nonetheless, he concluded his speech with an appeal that the program of the Equal Rights Association be enacted, observing: "The only safety for republican institutions is to be found in the ballot placed in the hands of all, without regard to color or sex."[56]

Douglass did more than just plead for the association's program. He joined Lucretia Mott, Susan B. Anthony, Elizabeth Cady Stanton, and Lucy Stone in petitioning the New York Constitutional Convention to amend the state constitution so "as to secure the right of suffrage to all citizens, without distinction of race or sex." Along with Henry Ward Beecher and Stanton, Douglass was appointed an association representative to the Constitutional Convention to argue for the elimination of the $250 property qualification for Negro suffrage and for the extension of the franchise to women.[57] In December 1866, Douglas helped draft a memorial to Congress on behalf of the Equal Rights Association, protesting any change in the U.S. Constitution or any legislation by Congress "which shall longer violate the principle of Republican government, by proscriptive distinctions in rights of suffrage and citizenship, on account of color or sex."[58]

But the areas of cooperation were rapidly narrowing. Many of the women in the association, led by Stanton and Anthony, were incensed by the Republican party's indifference to their demands for woman suffrage and attributed it to the influence of a number of former abolitionists. In their anger—an anger not too difficult to understand in view of the historic discrimination against women—they not only began to claim priority for woman suffrage, but announced that they were ready to make common cause with any group, even those opposed to Negro suffrage.

It was this change that led Anthony to join forces with a wealthy reformer—the eccentric George Francis Train—when he offered to finance a weekly magazine, *The Revolution.* The weekly was to be managed by her and edited by Elizabeth Cady Stanton and Parker Pillsbury. Calling itself the "organ of the National Party of New America," *The Revolution* sought simultaneously to embrace all the emerging reform currents of the time: temperance and labor reform, practical education, free trade, and currency reform. In the area of politics, it called for an "educated suffrage, irrespective of sex or color; equal pay for equal work; eight hours for labor; abolition of standing armies and party despotism."[59]

Douglass agreed with a number of the demands advocated by *The Revolution,* such as labor reform, equal pay to women for equal work, and an eight-hour day. But he was disturbed by the emphasis the first issue placed on the need for an "educated suffrage." He grew increasingly angry as, in succeeding issues, Stanton and Anthony voiced agreement with the anti-Negro *New York Herald* that the educated white woman was more fit to be entrusted with the ballot than the "brutish and ignorant Negro who has been invested with political power" by the radical Republican Reconstruction legislation.[60] To his dismay, women who had once been active abolitionists agreed, in letters to *The Revolution,* with the magazine's editorial opinion that before the "ignorant black man" should be given the ballot, intelligent and cultured white women should be enfranchised. The Negro male must not "march to liberty over woman's prostrate form" became the slogan of the women who joined with Stanton and Anthony. In advancing this plea, they went so far as to appeal to southerners to support their cause on the ground that enfranchisement of women would provide a bulwark against "Negro rule" in the South.[61] Henry B. Blackwell, Lucy Stone's husband and a contributor to *The Revolution,* even dispatched an open letter to southern legislatures in which he set out to prove that, by granting suffrage to women, the combined white vote would be increased sufficiently to defeat the combined black vote; thus, "the Negro question would be forever removed from the political arena."[62] Parker Pillsbury not only endorsed this position, but argued in *The Revolution* that the Negro male, unlike women, did not deserve the ballot. While women had been active in the anti-slavery cause before the Civil War, he said, free black men had been indifferent to the struggle to loose the chains that bound their brothers and sisters in bondage.[63]

Douglass was well aware of the women's bitterness that a golden opportunity was slipping through their fingers. At the second anniversary of the Equal Rights Association in May 1868, he attempted to assuage their feelings. There had never been an hour, he told them, in which he had denied the right of women to the ballot. He shared their desire for a quick victory, but practical realities demanded that they hold off for a while. The great danger was that linking woman suffrage with Negro suffrage would seriously lessen the chances of securing the ballot for black men, and to the Negro, he reiterated, the ballot was "an urgent necessity." The people were ready to listen to the Negro's claim, but they still remained to be convinced of the necessity for woman suffrage. Why, then, jeopardize the real possibility of securing Negro suffrage by making it dependent upon the achievement of woman suffrage? In ten years, in five years, perhaps in three, it would be the woman's hour. But Gettysburg and Atlanta had not been fought on the woman question.

While many of the women were unmoved by Douglass's arguments, they joined the others in reelecting him a vice-president of the association.[64]

Douglass reiterated his position later in the year at the Boston Woman's Convention. This time he stressed the point that the achievement of woman suffrage "depended upon the preliminary success of Negro suffrage." The reporter for *The Independent* noted that Douglass "shone; all the revolutionary fire broke out" as he advanced this argument. But Lucy Stone was unconvinced and vigorously disagreed with Douglass.[65]

The white feminists were certainly not unaware of the thrust of Douglass's argument. They had seen how the southern state legislatures, operating under the Reconstruction policies of President Andrew Johnson, had been dominated by former slaveholders; how they had expressed regret that the South had been forced by military defeat to abolish slavery; how they refused to confer citizenship upon the ex-slaves, barred them from voting, and denied them any place in the political life of the South, while at the same time adopting legislation such as the Black Codes, which bound Negroes to the land on which they worked and all but reenslaved them. They were familiar, too, with the fearsome reports that Negroes who dared to protest were being lynched by the Ku Klux Klan and other extralegal organizations and that hundreds of blacks were being massacred in anti-Negro riots in Memphis, New Orleans, and other southern cities. These tragic events, which threatened to wipe out the gains of the Emancipation Proclamation and the Thirteenth Amendment, had led even moderates in the North to see the critical necessity of the Negro vote to safeguard the legal freedom the ex-slaves had secured during the Civil War. What Douglass feared was that the linking of woman suffrage to Negro (male) suffrage would destroy the moderate-radical coalition which alone could protect the ex-slaves from a state of quasi-slavery. Hence, he joined forces with former abolitionists and radical and moderate Republicans in seeking the adoption of a constitutional amendment which would guarantee the ex-slaves access to the ballot box. He had now reluctantly concluded that the only chance of passage lay in separating it from the fight for woman suffrage.

On February 25, 1869, after receiving the necessary two-thirds vote in both houses of Congress, the Fifteenth Amendment was submitted to the state legislatures. Douglass was jubilant, and intensified his agitation to secure ratification. From platforms all over the North, he repeated his message that the nation's interest would best be served by guaranteeing the Negro's right to the ballot. He called on the veterans of the anti-slavery struggle to lend their influence to the campaign for the ratification of the new amendment.

From one quarter, his appeal met with a painful rebuff. Susan B. Anthony, Elizabeth Cady Stanton, and many of their followers were enraged that the amendment did not include a provision barring discrimination at the ballot box because of sex, as well as race or color. They accused Douglass of pushing one reform at the expense of another, of advancing Negro suffrage and neglecting woman suffrage. The Fifteenth Amendment "cannot with justice be passed," wrote Stanton in *The Revolution*.[66]

A heated controversy arose between Douglass and the feminists at the annual meeting of the Equal Rights Association in New York early in May 1869. Douglass argued earnestly that white women were entitled to the ballot and expressed his regret that they had not been included in the amendment. But he insisted that they must understand that his people were confronted by special problems. "When women," he said, "because they are women, are dragged from their houses and hung upon lamp-posts; when their children are torn from their arms, and their brains dashed upon the pavement; when they are objects of insult and outrage at every turn; when they are in danger of having their homes burnt down over their heads; when their children are not allowed to enter schools; then they will have an urgency to obtain the ballot equal to our own." When someone in the audience shouted, "Is that not all true about black women?" Douglass replied: "Yes, yes, yes; it is true of the black woman, but not because she is a woman, but because she is black." Women, he said, had many ways to redress their grievances; the Negro had only one.

The answering arguments by Susan B. Anthony and Lucy Stone revealed that they were by now fully convinced that the task of implementing the freedom of the Negro in the South had to be subordinated to the cause of white women. Anthony argued that "if intelligence, justice, and morality are to have precedence in the government, then let the question of women be brought up first and that of the Negro last." Stone insisted that woman suffrage was more imperative than voting rights of Negroes. She spoke of the "Ku-Kluxes here in the North in the shape of men who take away the children from the mother and separate them as completely as if done on the block of the auctioneer." Still, she was willing to favor passage of the amendment if it could not be changed to include women: "I will be thankful in my soul if *any* body can get out of the terrible pit."

However, in the case of Anthony, Stanton, and the vast majority of the white women delegates there could be no compromise. Anthony had already pledged that "I will cut off this right arm of mine before I will work for or demand the ballot for the negro and not the woman." Stanton had warned in *The Revolution* that manhood suffrage alone would create "an antagonism between black men and all women that will culminate in fearful outrages on womanhood, especially in the South." They and their supporters did not hesitate to raise a barrage of derogatory epithets against black men, referring to them as "Sambos" and "ignorant barbarians" who were a menace to black as well as white women and would become more so if enfranchised.

While Douglass replied sharply to the slurs cast upon black men, he still tried to prevent the breach from becoming worse. He introduced a resolution stating that the association "hails the extension of suffrage to any class heretofore disfranchised, as a cheering part of the triumph of the whole idea" and that the delegates "gratefully welcome the pending fifteenth amendment, prohibiting disfranchisement on account of race, and earnestly solicit the State Legislatures to pass it without delay." Douglas read with special emphasis that section of his resolution which spoke of the amendment as the "culmination of one-half of our demands" and called for the redoubling "of our energy to secure the further amendment guaranteeing the same sacred rights without limitation to sex." But the majority of the women were not impressed. They retaliated by asserting "that until the constitution shall know neither black nor white, neither male nor female, but only the equal rights of all classes, we renew our solemn indictment against that instrument as defective, unworthy, and an oppressive charter for the self-government of a free people."[67]

The feminists who dominated the convention were quite prepared to see the Fifteenth Amendment go down to defeat rather than support a measure which did not include the enfranchisement of women. Before the meeting adjourned, they dissolved the Equal Rights Association and formed the National Woman's Suffrage Association, which divorced itself completely from the question of Negro suffrage.

Douglass was the leading figure in the futile effort to convince the woman's rights leaders that they should support the Fifteenth Amendment, even though it did not include the right to vote for women. But he was not alone. William Lloyd Garrison, Wendell Phillips, Horace Greeley, Gerrit Smith, and other white anti-slavery and "woman's rights men" supported his position, as did black men active in the abolitionist and woman's causes, such as Charles Lenox Remond, Robert Purvis, George T. Downing, and Lewis Hayden. So, too, did Julia Ward Howe, author of the "Battle Hymn of the Republic," Lydia Maria Child, an outstanding abolitionist leader, Mary Ashton Livermore, woman's rights leader in Illinois, Frances Dana Gage, Ohio abolitionist, and Lucy Stone. Stone broke with her husband, Henry B. Blackwell, who strongly opposed ratification of the Fifteenth Amendment. Lydia Maria Child publicly rebuked Stanton and her colleagues for denouncing the Negro's right to vote in "the sneering tone habitually assumed by slaveholders and their copperhead allies" and for being willing "to sacrifice the rights of colored men in order to secure the cooperation of Southern men in their efforts for the enfranchisement of woman." She pointedly asked:

Shall our influence go to strengthen the murderous hands of
the Ku-Klux-Klan? If we think *our* rights would be more per-
fectly secured if we were allowed to vote, how much more
true is it of *them*, who are living in the midst of cunning and
malignant enemies! I regard it as a shame to womanhood
that any one should think of bartering away their rights for
the sake of more promptly securing her own.[68]

As for herself, she said: "I am glad that we shall come in after the
negro, whose wrongs and sufferings, patiently borne, have made
him in our eyes an august, a heroic personage."[69]

Mary Ashton Livermore refused to publish articles by Anthony
and Stanton on the Fifteenth Amendment in her paper, *The Agitator*,
because they called upon women to oppose the amendment and
demeaned the Negro male's right to the suffrage. She assured black
Americans that

the Western women moving for woman's enfranchisement,
do *not* oppose the Fifteenth Amendment. We have never heard
it opposed at a Western women's meeting, in a single instance.
Western women comprehend that humanity is one—that the
colored man cannot be elevated without, at the same time,
uplifting the colored woman—and they see clearly that through
the gap in the fence made by the colored man, as he passes
over into citizenship, all American women will pass to the
same destination.

She made this statement, moreover, after visits to woman's rights
conventions in Illinois, Indiana, Ohio, Michigan, Kansas, and Wis-
consin.[70]

At a Woman's Rights Convention in Chicago in September 1869,
Lucy Stone introduced the resolution declaring the women's support for the Fifteenth Amendment and asserted that "we rejoice
in every extension of suffrage." The resolution was carried with
only two dissenting votes. Stone declared that the vote was

an accurate expression of the feeling of the woman's suffrage
advocates in regard to the Fifteenth Amendment. Not one in a
thousand of them is opposed to it. On the contrary, they know

that negro men, and all women, suffer a grievous, common wrong, and are glad when either class, or individuals of either class, can escape from it. Let the friends of both causes cheerfully give each other credit for real facts. Each bitterly needs all the help of the other.[71]

Writing in *The Woman's Advocate*, Frances Dana Gage announced her disagreement with Stanton and Anthony, with whom she had collaborated for years:

Could I with breath defeat the Fifteenth Amendment, I would not do it. That Amendment will let the colored men enter the wide portals of human rights. Keeping them out, suffering as now, would not let me in all the sooner, then in God's name why stand in their way? It is my earnest wish that the Fifteenth Amendment may be ratified. Let us apply the Golden Rule now and forever.[72]

The position of black women was voiced by Frances Ellen Watkins Harper, the distinguished poet, novelist, anti-slavery lecturer, and woman's rights advocate. Her speech to the white women at the 1869 meeting of the American Equal Rights Association was described in these words:

When it is a question of race, she let the lesser question of sex go. But the white women all go for sex, letting race occupy a minor position. . . . If the nation could handle only one question, she would not have the black women put a single straw in the way, if only the men of the race could obtain what they wanted.[73]

All this made no impression on Stanton, Anthony, and their followers. Women, wrote Stanton, had "too much pride, self-respect, and womanly dignity" to rejoice in the adoption of the Fifteenth Amendment. While she felt that many of the "woman's rights men" had betrayed the trust placed in them by women, she was particularly bitter over Douglass's retreat from the position he had espoused in the early stages of the American Equal Rights Association, especially since he had been the first among the "woman's rights men" to advocate woman's right to the ballot. Stanton made this clear when she wrote that "common-sense women . . . felt towards the Fifteenth Amendment, which places all women under the heels of all men, precisely as Mr. Douglass would have felt had it proposed to enfranchise the men of all races but his own."[74]

Douglass viewed this attack as proof that women like Elizabeth Cady Stanton simply did not understand the special problems facing black Americans in the crucial years immediately following the Civil War. He regretted that he had to part company with many women who were his personal friends and with whom he had worked so closely for thirty years. But he was comforted by the knowledge that the Fifteenth Amendment was being ratified by state after state and that especially in the West, women active in the woman's cause had been involved in petitioning the state legislatures, urging ratification. In a speech in Boston on December 25, 1869, Douglass expressed his gratitude to these women. Then, describing his elation at the victories gained by the anti-slavery cause, he went on to remind the men and women present that the battle was not over, for women had yet to gain the vote. "Women are entitled to the ballot, alike by right, and by the Republican government here assumed to exist," he declared. To thunderous applause, he vowed that once the Fifteenth Amendment became part of the law of the land, he would devote himself to the struggle to gain the vote for women.[75]

On March 30, 1870, President Ulysses S. Grant proclaimed the adoption of the Fifteenth Amendment. Celebrations were the order of the day. Amid the rejoicing, Douglass did not forget his pledge to the women of America. He called for the immediate organization of a campaign for a new amendment to the Constitution, granting woman suffrage, and he advised black women to prepare themselves, "when the sixteenth amendment becomes law, to cooperate in the various schemes which will be presented to their favor."[76] Eager to show women that they had not lost a champion, he devoted special attention to their cause in his new paper, *The New National Era*, a weekly founded in Washington, D.C., in 1870. In one of his editorials, Douglass paised Victoria Claflin Woodhull for arguing that the Fourteenth and Fifteenth Amendments already gave women the suffrage.[77]

Victoria Woodhull and her sister, Tennessee Claflin, brokers on Wall Street and publishers of their famous *Weekly*, were ardent advocates of woman's rights and "social freedom." Victoria Wood-hull felt that the woman suffragists in the Stanton-Anthony camp had been wrong in splitting with Douglass, whom she admired and respected, and that the movement would be benefited by re-uniting the woman's struggle with the Negro's cause.

In May 1872, on a far-reaching platform which included the right of every person, male and female, to vote, Victoria Woodhull was nominated for President of the United States as the candidate of the Equal Rights party. Then, at her suggestion, Moses Hall of Louisiana nominated Frederick Douglass for Vice-President, declaring: "We have the oppressed race represented by Douglass." The delegates agreed, and welcomed Douglass as their vice-presidential candidate, after which, to the tune of "Coming Through the Rye," they sang:

> Yes! Victoria we've selected
>   For our chosen head;
> With Fred Douglass on the ticket
>   We will raise the dead.

The convention closed, hailing "The Woman's, Negro and Working-man's Ticket—Victoria Woodhull of New York for President; Frederick Douglass of the District of Columbia for Vice-President."[78]

Early in June, Woodhull accepted her nomination. But Douglass was too busy with personal affairs to notify the new party that he could not be its candidate. On June 2, his house in Rochester, New York, was burned to the ground. His wife, their daughter and son-in-law, and their three children managed to escape. But the furniture and Douglass's library, including twelve volumes (1848 to 1860) of *The North Star* and *Frederick Douglass' Paper*—the only complete file in existence—was destroyed.[79]

With her profession of free love, Victoria Woodhull offended many people, including the woman's rights leaders. She soon lost her influence, and she and her sister left the United States for Great Britain. But the point she had made about reuniting the woman's cause and that of the black American did not depart with her. By the fall of 1873, even though the resentment over the failure of the Fifteenth Amendment to enfranchise women was still bitter, the leaders of the woman suffrage movement were anxious to reconcile their differences with Douglass. Peace was restored at the 1876 convention of the National Woman Suffrage Association. Douglass had been invited to attend, and he came. While neither Stanton nor Anthony expressed any regret over their criticism of their former friend and ally, they made it clear that they needed his help in the continuing campaign for woman's rights. Douglass responded briefly and indicated that he still smarted from the way in which some woman's rights leaders had referred to black men as "ignorant, besotted creatures" during the heated battle over the Fifteenth Amendment. Nevertheless, he announced that he was "willing to be part of the bridge over which women should march to the full enjoyment of their rights."

Once the reconciliation had taken place, Douglass was again a familiar figure at women's rights conventions. In announcing the gatherings, *The Woman's Journal,* official organ of the National Woman Suffrage Association, always made sure to include the notice: "Among the Guests and Speakers will be Frederick Douglass." In 1885, Douglass placed woman suffrage second on the list of causes to which he wished to devote the rest of his life—the first, of course, being the continued struggle for the full freedom of his people. Indeed, he argued, the extension of the ballot to women was interrelated with the struggle "to redress the great injustice of our nation"— the continued oppression of black Americans. He brushed aside all arguments against woman's ability to use the vote intelligently, insisting: "I know of no class better equipped to manage the ballot than American women."[80]

In his appearances at woman suffrage conventions, Douglass always sought to encourage those disheartened that a constitutional amendment to enfranchise women, introduced in every session of Congress since 1869, had received little or no consideration. He reminded the women delegates that on many occasions before the Civil War the cause of the slave had also seemed hopeless. But by arousing and educating the people, the anti-slavery forces had triumphed. He had no doubt that the woman's cause, a truly just one, was bound to triumph; it required only persistent agitation and organization. He reminded the delegates that, as far back as 1853, he had argued that women would never gain justice through the goodwill of men, no matter how "plain and simple" their cause. "What she desires," he emphasized, "she must fight for." And what she was fighting for, he pointed out, was of the utmost importance to society. In 1885, Douglass wrote to a friend that he found the woman's rights meetings "a substitute for the old time anti-slavery meetings." Even more, he told the women at these meetings that he regarded their movement to be more important than the movement to end slavery, significant though that had been, because their struggle "comprehends the liberation and elevation of one-half of the whole human family," and "if successful, it will be the most stupendous revolution the world has ever witnessed."[81]

Not all who were associated with the woman's movement were happy over Douglass's return to their ranks and over the publicity his appearances received in the press. Southern suffragists had begun to organize in the 1880s, and they grew increasingly annoyed with the northern suffragists for extending so warm a welcome to a black man. Southern politicians, they were convinced, would never enfranchise women if a Negro was too prominent in the cause. In December 1894, a South Carolina politician friendly to woman suffrage agreed to speak for the suffragists in Atlanta. In a letter to a leader of the movement in his state, he wrote: "You are a Southern woman and can appreciate the feeling of our people. In Woman Suffrage meetings up North, Fred Douglass has been a great card I believe. It would be well enough for him not to be at Atlanta. This of course is confidential between us."[82]

Douglass was never invited to attend a meeting of a southern suffrage association, but he remained a welcome visitor to meetings of the leading women's organizations in every other part of the country. On every occasion, as speaker and writer, he paid tribute to the contributions of women to the struggle for a more democratic America. Shortly before his death, he listed the departed veterans of the woman's rights movement—Lucretia Mott, Ernestine L. Rose, Angelina Grimké, Lucy Stone, and others—as among "the best of mankind," and said: "No good cause can fail when supported by such women."[83] In nearly every speech he delivered, in every article he wrote for a magazine or newspaper, in every one of his three autobiographies, he included a tribute to women, black and white.

On the afternoon of February 20, 1895, Douglass left his home at Cedar Hill, in Anacostia, to attend a meeting of the National Council of Women in Washington. He returned home shortly after five o'clock for his dinner and planned to deliver a lecture that evening at the Hilldale African Church near his home. After dinner, he sat talking to his second wife, Helen Pitts Douglass, herself an active suffragist, about the events of the day at the Women's Council. Suddenly he fell to his knees. His heart had failed, and the greatest black American of the nineteenth century passed away quickly without regaining consciousness.

Newspapers in the United States and Europe carried the news of Douglass's death on their front pages. While many headlined the news with statements such as "Greatest Negro Leader Dead," some featured the report under the headline, "Friend and Champion of Women Dies." Not a few carried the statement Elizabeth Cady Stanton made in a letter to Susan B. Anthony which was to be read at memorial services for Douglass:

> He was the only man I ever saw who understood the degrada-
> tion of the disenfranchisement of women. Through all the long
> years of our struggle he has been a familiar figure on our plat-
> form with always an inspiring word to say. In the very first
> convention, he helped me to carry the resolution I had penned
> demanding woman suffrage. Frederick Douglass is not dead.
> His grand character will long be an object lesson in our Na-
> tional history. His lofty sentiments of liberty, justice and
> equality, echoed on every platform over our broad land, must
> influence and inspire many coming generations.[84]

*The Woman's Journal* of March 2, 1895, devoted five and one-quarter columns to his obituary. After noting that Douglass had spent his last day "in attendance at the National Council of Women, where he had been warmly welcomed and escorted to the platform," the article observed that it was "difficult to condense into an obituary notice even the most salient incidents of his picturesque and varied career. He was perhaps without exception the most striking example ever known of the ability of a human being to overcome the obstacles in his path to eminence and usefulness. His rise was far greater than that of Lincoln, for he had to overcome not only poverty, but chattel slavery, enforced illiteracy, race proscription, and lifelong social distinctions." Following a detailed presentation of the main facts in Douglass's long life, the article concluded:

One of the finest incidents in his career was his early and life-long espousal of the woman suffrage cause. Although half white, he was identified by social prejudice with the negro race, and his advocacy of race equality was inevitable. But his association with those peerless anti-slavery women speakers and workers—Sarah and Angelina Grimké, Abby Kelley, L. Maria Child, Maria Weston Chapman, Lucy Stone, Sarah Otis Ernst and others, and his recognition of their heroic and efficient services, made him at once and forever a woman suffragist. He was a speaker in the first woman's rights convention, with Mrs. Stanton at Seneca Falls, in 1848. He was a friend of Susan B. Anthony, and a member of both the American and the National Woman Suffrage Association. He spoke repeatedly for the Massachusetts and New England Conventions, and spent the last day of his life in attendance on the National Council of Women.

The news of Douglass's death reached the delegates of the National Council of Women as they were opening their evening session on February 20. Mary Wright Sewall, the presiding officer, adjourned the meeting, but before the hall was darkened, she told the hushed women:

> Surely it will be regarded as an historic coincidence that the man who, in his own person, embodied the history of almost a century, in the struggle between freedom and oppression, should have spent his last day as a witness of the united efforts of those who have come from so many different places and along such various avenues, to formulate some plan upon which they may unite to demand a new expression of freedom in the relation of woman to the world, to society, and to the state; and in the application of woman's brain and conscience to the great questions pending at this hour.[85]

Douglass would have appreciated this comment. He himself had once said that "in some respects the woman suffrage movement is but a continuance of the old anti-slavery movement." It was fitting that the end should have found him in the ranks of those who were carrying on this tradition.

Five state legislatures adopted resolutions of regret at the news of Douglass's death. The fact that one was North Carolina's angered a number of southern white suffragists. Carrie Chapman Catt, who had become head of the American Suffrage Association in 1892, was so upset by these tributes to Douglass that she wrote in March 1895:

I fear very much the success of the Southern work. I believe the field was in fair condition to do something, but the relation of our leaders to the colored question at the Douglas [sic] funeral, has completely taken the wind out of our sails. You should see some of the clippings I have from the Southern press and some of the letters. They were a little suspicious of us all along, but now they know we are abolitionists in disguise, with no other thought than to set the negro in dominance over them. It was a bad case and I do not know how we are going to get out of it.[86]

But neither Mrs. Catt nor her correspondents voiced the true sentiments of women, black and white, about the contributions of this nineteenth-century giant to their cause. These were much more accurately expressed at the Memorial Meeting in Philadelphia on April 15, 1895, by Mrs. Fannie Jackson Coppin, leader of the woman's rights movement in the Quaker city. In delivering one of the eulogies, she said: "We have lost the most conspicuous advocate of our rights, by the death of Frederick Douglass."[87]

## NOTES

1. *The Liberator*, September 13, 1834.
2. Ibid., October 6, 1837.
3. Ibid., December 14, 1838, November 29, 1839.
4. Gilbert H. Barnes, *The Anti-Slavery Impulse* (New York, 1933), p. 43.
5. *The Liberator*, March 14, 1835. The petitions became so numerous and continuous and led to so much controversy that in 1836 the House of Representatives voted to table henceforth all consideration of petitions on the subject.
6. Barnes, op. cit., p. 140. Caleb Cushing (1800-1879), lawyer and statesman, Whig member of the U.S. House of Representatives (1835-1843), special envoy to China to negotiate treaties and open Chinese ports to American trade, U.S. Attorney-General (1853-1857).

7. *New York Sun* editorial reprinted in *The Liberator*, September 15, 1837.

8. *The Liberator*, July 7, 1837. For an excellent biography, see Gerda Lerner, *The Grimke Sisters from South Carolina: Pioneers for Woman's Rights and abolition* (New York, 1968).

9. Samuel J. May, *Some Recollections of Our Anti-Slavery Conflict* (Boston, 1869), pp. 237-238.

10. Gilbert H. Barnes and Dwight L. Dumond, eds., *Weld-Grimké Correspondence. Letters of Theodore H. Weld, Angelina Grimké Weld, Sarah Grimke* (New York 1934), vol. II, pp. 415, 424, 428, 441.

11. *The Liberator*, March 28, 1838.

12. Ibid., May 23, 1839.

13. Ibid., July 19, 1839.

14. Barnes, op. cit., pp. 153-160.

15. *National Anti-Slavery Standard*, March 6, 1840.

16. Philip S. Foner, *Frederick Douglass* (New York, 1962), pp. 15-27.

17. Douglass published the details of the purchase of his freedom, including the bill of sale, in his paper, *The North Star*, December 13, 1847, and prefaced it with the following comment: "We give our readers the evidence of our right to be free in this democratic and Christian country—not so much however to establish our right to ourself as to expose the cold-blooded Methodist man-stealer, who claimed us as his property, and the hypocritical nation that has sanctioned his infamous claim."

18. Douglass to Julia Griffiths, October 13, 1847, Douglass *Mss.*, Frederick Douglass Papers, Library of Congress, Washington, D.C.

19. Adelaide Elizabeth Dorn, "A History of the Anti-Slavery Movement in Rochester and Vicinity," unpublished M.A. thesis, University of Buffalo, 1949, pp. 49-51.

20. Frederick Douglass, *Life and Times of Frederick Douglass* (Hartford, Conn., 1881), p. 242; *Frederick Douglass' Paper*, January 9, 1854.

21. *The North Star*, March 9, 1849.

22. *Pennsylvania Freeman*, August 22, 1844; *New York Herald*, September 12, 1852; *The North Star*, December 5, 1847.

23. Elizabeth Cady Stanton, Susan B. Anthony, and Matilda Joslyn Gage, eds., *History of Woman Suffrage* (New York, 1881), vol. I, pp. 70-71.

24. Ibid., p. 73; *The Woman's Journal*, April 14, 1888, p. 116.

25. *The Woman's Journal*, April 14, 1888, p. 116; Mary Church Terrell, "Frederick Douglass," *Centennial Anniversary of Seneca county and Auxiliary Papers*, Seneca Falls Historical Society (Seneca Falls, New York, 1908), p. 55.

26. Stanton, Anthony, Gage, op. cit., vol. I, p. 86; *The North Star*, August 11, 1848. Mrs. Stanton and Lucretia Mott had proposed Douglass as the chairman of the meeting, but the women of Rochester had opposed the suggestion and elected Abigail Rush, a local resident, to the office.

27. *New York Tribune*, October 23-25, 1850; Harriet Jane Robinson, *Massachusetts in the Woman Suffrage Movement* (Boston, 1881), p. 25.

28. *New York Herald*, October 23, 1850; *New York Mirror*, October 24, 1850. The *Rochester Daily American* of December 16, 1850, referred to the "She-Socialists" who had been prominent in the convention.

29. Douglass to Gerrit Smith, January 1, 1856, Gerrit Smith Papers, George Arents Research Library, Syracuse University; Susan B. Anthony to Gerrit Smith, December 25, 1855, ibid.; *Frederick Douglass' Paper*, July 18, 1859; Helen T. Shea, "The Woman's Rights Movement in New York State, 1848-1854," unpublished M.A. thesis, Columbia University, 1940, p. 15.

30. *Frederick Douglass' Paper*, June 10, 1853; Shea, op. cit., pp. 31-35.

31. *Frederick Douglass' Paper*, November 25, December 16, 1853.

32. *Frederick Douglass' Paper*, February 10, 1854. The plan for an industrial school never materialized.

33. *The North Star*, July 28, 1848; *Frederick Douglass' Paper*, February 17, March 17, 1854; *The Liberator*, April 6, 1855. Lucy Stone defended her conduct, noting that she had protested the exclusion before the meeting started and went ahead nonetheless. Her defense did not persuade Douglass or other blacks (*Frederick Douglass' Paper*, March 10, 1853).

34. *Douglass' Monthly*, October 1859.

35. See, for example, letters of Chas. L. Reason and J. H. Langston in *Frederick Douglass' Paper*, February 10, December 1, 1854.

36. *The Alienated American* (Cleveland), April 9, 1853.

37. *The Liberator*, November 18, 1853.

38. *National Anti-Slavery Standard*, September 24, 1853. The question, however, had been privately discussed. In January 1852, Samuel D. Porter, a Rochester anti-slavery associate, had warned Douglass that the city was "full of scandalous reports" concerning his relations with Julia Griffiths. Douglass had emphatically denied that there was anything in these relations that should cause him to feel ashamed and expressed resentment that his close friend had given even slight credence to the rumors (Douglass to Samuel D. Porter, January 12, 1852, Samuel D. Porter Papers, University of Rochester Library).

39. *The Liberator*, December 2, 15, 1853.

40. *Frederick Douglass' Paper*, December 9, 1853.

41. *Saturday Visitor*, reprinted in *The Liberator*, January 13, 1854. James B. Vashon, a black leader in Pittsburgh, denounced Garrison for his "savage attack" upon Julia Griffiths, "an innocent female, whose humanity caused her to leave her native country," and who had consistently proved to be a "true fighter against oppression," (*Frederick Douglass Paper*, January 13, 1854).

42. Susan B. Anthony to William Lloyd Garrison, December 13, 1853, Anti-Slavery Letters to Garrison, Boston Public Library.

43. Rosetta Douglass Sprague, *Anna Murray Douglass: My Mother as I Recall Her. Delivered Before the Anna Murray Douglass Union W.C.T.U. Washington, D.C., 1900* (reprinted Washington, D.C., 1923), pp. 12-14.

44. Douglass to Mrs. Lydia Dennett, April 17, 1857, *Ms.,* Houghton Division, Harvard University Library.

45. Douglass to Doctress S. M. Loguen, August 12, 1882, *Ms.,* Howard University Library.

46. Sprague, op. cit., pp. 21-22.

47. Lucretia Mott to Elizabeth Cady Stanton, October 3, 1848, Elizabeth Cady Stanton Papers, Library of Congress, Manuscripts Division, Washington, D.C.

48. Douglass to Gerrit Smith, July 15, 1853, Gerrit Smith Papers, George Arents Research Library, Syracuse University.

49. *Douglass' Monthly,* November 1860; S. S. Foster to Gerrit Smith, August 25, 1860, Gerrit Smith Papers, George Arents Research Library, Syracuse University.

50. *The Liberator,* October 22, 1858. Douglass's resolutions, never adopted because the mob broke up the meeting, emphasized that life belonged to God only and the State had no right to deprive any one of it, and that instead of barbarously taking away the life of a criminal, "we should urge a thorough reform in our criminal laws—basing them on the truly Christian principle of love and good will towards man, and to reject forever the cold-blooded and barbarous principle of retaliation" (ibid).

51. *The Liberator,* February 10, 1865.

52. *National Anti-Slavery Standard,* December 30, 1865. For the role played by woman's rights leaders, especially Elizabeth Cady Stanton and Susan B. Anthony, in achieving the Thirteenth Amendment, see James M. McPherson, *The Struggle for Equality: Abolitionists and the Negro in the Civil War and Reconstruction* (Princeton, N.J., 1964), pp. 125-26.

53. *National Anti-Slavery Standard,* February 17, 1866.

54. *New York Tribune,* May 12, 1866.

55. *New York Herald,* November 21, 1866.

56. *New York Tribune, New York Herald,* November 21, 1866.

57. Susan B. Anthony to Douglass, December 15, 1866; Elizabeth Cady Stanton to Douglass, January 8, 1867, Frederick Douglass Papers, Library of Congress, Manuscripts Division, Washington, D.C.

58. *National Anti-Slavery Standard,* December 22, 1866.

59. *The Revolution,* January 8, 1868; Katherine Anthony, *Susan B. Anthony: Her Personal History and Her Era* (New York, 1954), p. 215; Alma Lutz, *Susan B. Anthony: Rebel, Crusader, Humanitarian* (Boston, 1959), pp. 38-39.

60. *New York Herald,* July 4, 1868; *The Revolution,* July 11, 1868.

61. *The Revolution,* December 3, 1868.

62. Henry B. Blackwell, *What the South Can Do* (New York, January 1867).

63. *The Revolution*, September 7, 1869.

64. Ibid., May 21, 1868.

65. *The Independent*, November 26, 1868.

66. *The Revolution*, April 9, 1869.

67. *The Revolution*, May 20, 27, 1869; Eleanor Flexner, *Century of Struggle. The Woman's Rights Movement in the United States* (Cambridge, Mass., 1959), pp. 142-146; Robert E. Riegel, The Split of the Feminist Movement in 1869," *Mississippi Valley Historical Review* 49 (1962-1963):485-496; Aileen S. Kraditor, *The Ideas of the Woman Suffrage Movement 1890-1920* (New York, 1965), pp. 167-168.

68. *National Anti-Slavery Standard*, June 6, 1868, August 21, 1869.

69. Ibid., November 28, 1868, August 28, 1869.

70. *The Woman's Advocate*, July 10, 1869, reprinted in *National Anti-Slavery Standard*, July 17, 1869.

71. *National Anti-Slavery Standard*, September 25, 1869.

72. *The Woman's Advocate*, August, 1869.

73. *The Revolution*, May 17, 1869.

74. Ibid., May 27, 1869.

75. *National Anti-Slavery Standard*, December 29, 1869.

76. *The New Era*, May 12, 1870. Writing in *The Revolution* of May 19, 1870, Parker Pillsbury made no reference to Douglass's pledge to continue the battle for woman suffrage, but, instead, accused black men, in their celebrations marking the ratification of the Fifteenth Amendment, of having forgotten the woman's cause. Nowhere had there been "the least recognition of woman."

77. *The New National Era*. September 21, 1871. A black woman correspondent insisted that the Fifteenth Amendment enfranchised black women since it stated: "The right of citizens to vote shall not be denied on account of race, color, or previous condition of servitude." She noted: "It does not say, 'the right of male citizens to vote,' &c., but says 'citizens.'" "It is a gross injustice that the colored women have so long been defrauded of their right to vote," she concluded, urging Douglass to take the lead in a drive to have the Fifteenth Amendment applied to black women (Mary Olney Brown in *The New National Era*, October 24, 1872).

78. *Woodhull & Claflin's Weekly*, May 18, June 1, 1872.

79. Douglass was fairly certain that the fire was "the work of an incendiary." Referring to his having been denied shelter at the Congress Hall in Rochester when he returned home upon being notified of the fire, he informed his readers: "I may be wrong, but I fear that the sentiment which repelled me at Congress Hall burnt my house" (Foner, *Frederick Douglass*, p. 302).

80. Elizabeth Cady Stanton, Susan B. Anthony, and Frances Gage, *History of Woman Suffrage* (New York, 1886), vol. III, p. 7; *The Woman's Journal*, December 1, 1888.

81. *The Woman's Journal*, June 2, 1888; undated Address before Woman Suffrage Convention, Douglass *Mss.*, Library of Congress, Manuscripts Division, Washington, D.C.; Douglass to Oliver Johnson, 1884, ibid.

82. Robert R. Hemphill to My dear Madam, Columbia, S.C., December 10, 1894, *Ms.*, Cleveland Historical Society.

83. *The Woman's Journal*, March 24, 1894.

84. See *Washington Evening Star*, February 25, 1895, and *Brooklyn Daily Eagle*, February 25, 1895. Susan B. Anthony remained with Douglass's widow throughout the entire day following his death. Benjamin Quarles, "Frederick Douglass and the Woman's Rights Movement," *Journal of Negro History*, 25 (1940) p. 44.

85. *The Woman's Journal*, March 2, 1895.

86. Carrie Chapman Catt to Mrs. Blake, New York, March 7, 1895, *Ms.*, Cleveland Historical Society.

87. *In Memoriam Frederick Douglass* (Philadelphia, 1897), p. 241.

# 1    THE WOMAN'S CAUSE

## WOMAN

By nature, she is fitted to occupy a position as elevated and digni-fied as her self-created master. And though she is often treated by him as his drudge, or a convenient piece of household furniture, 'tis but a striking evidence of his mental imbecility and moral de-pravity.

*The North Star,* May 26, 1848

## THE LADIES

The almoners of the race of man, superior to the opposite sex in all the offices of benevolence and kindness, fully equal in moral, mental and intellectual endowments, in short, entitled to an equal participancy in all the designs and accomplishments allotted to man during his career on earth. May the accumulated evils of the past, and those of the present, which superstition and bigotry have prescribed for them as a test of inferiority, be buried forever.

*The North Star,* August 10, 1848

## THE RIGHTS OF WOMEN

One of the most interesting events of the past week, was the holding of what is technically styled a Woman's Rights Convention at Seneca Falls. The speaking, addresses, and resolutions of this extraordinary meeting was wholly conducted by women; and although they evidently felt themselves in a novel position, it is but simple justice to say that their whole proceedings were characterized by marked ability and dignity. No one present, we think, however much he might be disposed to differ from the views advanced by the leading speakers on that occasion, will fail to give them credit for brilliant talents and excellent dispositions. In this meeting, as in other deliberative assemblies, there were frequent differences of opinion and animated discussion; but in no case was there the slightest absence of good feeling and decorum. Several interesting documents setting forth the rights as well as the grievances of women were read. Among these was a Declaration of Sentiments, to be regarded as the basis of a grand movement for attaining the civil, social, political, and religious rights of women. We should not do justice to our own convictions, or to the excellent persons connected with this infant movement, if we did not in this connection offer a few remarks on the general subject which the Convention met to consider and the objects they seek to attain. In doing so, we are not insensible that the bare mention of this truly important subject in any other than terms of contemptuous ridicule and scornful disfavor, is likely to excite against us the fury of bigotry and the folly of prejudice. A discussion of the rights of animals would be regarded with far more complacency by many of what are called the "wise" and the "good" of our land, than would a discussion of the rights of women. It is, in their estimation to be guilty of evil thoughts, to think that woman is entitled to equal rights with man. Many who have at last made the discovery that the negroes have some rights as well as other members of the human family, have yet to be convinced that women are entitled to any. Eight years ago a number of persons of this description actually abandoned the anti-slavery cause, lest by giving their influence in that direction they might possibly be giving countenance to the dangerous heresy that woman, in respect to rights, stands on an equal footing with man. In the judgment of such persons the American slave system, with all its concomitant horrors, is less to be deplored than this "wicked" idea. It is perhaps needless to say, that we cherish little sympathy for such sentiments or respect for such prejudices. Standing as we do up on the watch-tower of human freedom, we cannot be deterred from an expression of our approbation of any movement, however humble, to improve and elevate the character of any members of the human family. While it is impossible for us to go into this subject at length, and dispose of the various objections which are often urged against such a doctrine as that of female equality, we are free to say that in respect to political rights, we hold woman to be justly entitled to all we claim for man. We go farther, and express our conviction that all political rights which it is expedient for man to exercise, it is equally so for woman. All that distinguishes man as an intelligent and accountable being, is equally true of woman, and if that government only is just which governs by the free consent of the governed, there can be no reason in the world for denying to woman the exercise of the elective franchise, or a hand in making and administering the laws of the land. Our doctrine is that "right is of no sex." We therefore bid the women engaged in this movement our humble Godspeed.

*The North Star*, July 28, 1848

## THE ONLY TRUE BASIS OF RIGHTS
## REMARKS AT WOMAN'S RIGHTS CONVENTION
## ROCHESTER, NEW YORK, AUGUST 2, 1848

Frederick Douglass remarked that the only true basis of rights, was the capacity of individuals, and as for himself he dared not claim a right which he would not concede to women. In reference to the enfranchisement of women, it need not be questioned whether she would use that right or not; he contended that man should not withhold it from her; he alluded to the oppressive customs in the Old World, which so wronged woman, that they subjected her to the most laborious as well as degrading means for a livelihood. He would see her elevated to an equal position with man in every relation of life.

*The North Star*, August 11, 1848

## THE WOMEN'S ASSOCIATION OF PHILADELPHIA[1]

The intermediate time on Saturday was mainly spent in visiting the ladies connected with the "Women's Association." These ladies are devoting their energies to improve the condition and character of the oppressed at the North, as well as to the freedom of the enslaved at the South. They number only thirteen at present, and I believe do not desire to enlarge their association—having seen the folly of large but inactive associations for promoting moral and philanthropic objects.—These ladies share the confidence and esteem of the whole community, and can at any time obtain the aid and assistance of large numbers, when they lead the way, in measures of immediate practical importance. At present they are devoting their means to sustain *The North Star* believing that in this way they can most effectually aid the cause of freedom and improvement.

To these ladies *The North Star* has already been largely indebted for assistance in time of need. It was chiefly through them that a Fair was held in Philadelphia last winter, in aid of *The North Star;* and during our recent visit to that city, finding that the paper was in great need, they generously donated thirty-three dollars for its relief.

I expect in the course of a few weeks to lay before our readers an appeal from these ladies in behalf of their contemplated fair to be held this winter. It is certainly worthy of the sympathy and co-operation of all who wish well to the colored people of this country; and I have no doubt that it will receive a large share of encouragement.

*The North Star*, June 15, 1849

## OUR COLORED SISTERS

A letter from a lady connected with the Committee of the Fair informs us that the Committee have experienced serious difficulty to securing a suitable room in which to hold the Fair. Until the last few days they were relying on the promise of the proprietor of the Assembly Building, but this gentleman, on learning that the Fair was to be conducted by colored ladies, has refused to let his rooms for that purpose. When he made the promise he supposed that the parties who were to occupy them were white persons—and he now excuses his failure to fulfil his contract on that ground. This is but another illustration of that persecuting spirit that every where prevails in this land against the colored people; and is also another reason in favor of holding the contemplated Fair.

The ladies were informed, by this gentleman of his word, that if they could assure him that the Fair was to be under the management of white persons, the rooms were at their service. How unspeakably mean and disgraceful is this requirement! Colored persons, it seems, then, are not even to be encouraged in laboring for their own elevation, and for the freedom of their own brothers and sisters, unless their efforts are under the management of white persons! This is a new feature in the manifestation of the prejudice and hatred with which we have been so long and painfully regarded. But let not our sisters be disheartened by this shameful and fraudulent treatment; let them rather put forth greater exertion, and evince a more determined spirit in the only cause in which they are embarked. The opposition with which they meet should only tend to quicken their energies, and to double their diligence. The greater the obstacles with which they have to contend, the greater will be the victory when it is gained. Our transatlantic friends will see, in this new form of cruelty and injustice, a good reason for holding up the hands of that class who are the objects of such unnatural treatment. We say to our colored sisters in Philadelphia, BE FIRM—UNDAUNTED—AND PERSEVERE. You are not without friends; and the time will come when your righteous endeavors to ameliorate and improve your own condition, and to rescue from ignorance, and from the galling yoke of bondage, three millions of your countrymen, will be appreciated by the world, and crowned with success by a righteous God.

*The North Star*, November 16, 1849

## THE WOMAN'S TEMPERANCE CONVENTION

Chief among the matters of interest and importance in our city this week, are the proceedings of the Woman's Temperance Convention, at Corinthian Hall [Rochester]. The circumstance of women coming together, not as idle spectators, but as real actors in the scenes of a grand public demonstration in behalf of Temperance, would have, of itself in the present instance, aroused a clamor. But there was additional cause of excitement. It had been adroitly announced that the speakers on the occasion would appear in "Bloomer Costume,"[2] and, doubtless, this had its effect in three ways, to attract, to repel, and to make the Convention notorious. We have not space this week for anything like an account of this assemblage. But we set down the occasion as a creditable one, and worthy of high commendation. The Convention met on Tuesday morning, and was, we learn, wholly composed of ladies. Here it seems the business of the Convention was prepared. In the afternoon, gentlemen were admitted. Mrs. E. Stanton of Seneca Falls, was in the Chair, and Miss Susan B. Anthony, the Secretary, was reading a series of resolutions when we entered. At first, the ladies seemed to hesitate. They evidently felt the novelty of their position, and very naturally showed some embarrassment; but, fully convinced that they were there at the call of duty, they soon plied themselves to the work, and advocated Temperance with an eloquence, though in some respects different from man's, yet quite as appropriate as his. Mrs. Stanton, emphatically the standard-bearer of the assemblage, broke the path for her sisters in assailing a point which had been made against one resolution by several gentlemen. The resolution affirmed that those who were indifferent to the temperance movement were "more" guilty than the traffickers in ardent spirits. Mr. Benjamin Fish, and Mr. Wm. C. Bloss thought it a little absurd to set down a man as being a little better on account of direct perpetration of crime, and the latter gentleman suggested that the resolution should read, "alike guilty." This amendment met no favor among the women. It was voted down in a decided manner, so that the actual traffickers in ardent spirits were voted by the Convention as less guilty than those who are indifferent to the temperance movement. We were pleased to see that another amendment to the same resolution was warmly supported by the Convention, as it showed that the women assembled were of the right stamp.—The resolution contained the stereotype phrase, "our otherwise happy land." Mr. G. W. Clarke moved that this be struck out, for the reason that if Temperance should triumph tomorrow, this would be far from a happy land, if "three" million were, as they are held in chains. The amendment was carried.

The evening meeting was a fine one. The address delivered by Mrs. Stanton, was a brilliant production, and was listened to with marked attention throughout. The occasion was slightly marred by an ill-judged, but a well-intended movement, on the part of Mr. Stebbins, who ascended the platform and made a speech, which, though well enough in itself, was ill-timed, as coming after the able address of Mrs. Stanton.

The Convention did not separate till a "Woman's" State Temperance Society was formed, of which more hereafter.

*Frederick Douglass' Paper*, April 22, 1851

## WOMAN'S RIGHTS CONVENTION AT WORCESTER, MASS.

Absorbed as we are in these perilous times, with the great work of unchaining the American bondman, and assisting the hapless and hunted fugitive in his flight from his merciless pursuers to a place of safety, we have little time to consider the inequalities, wrongs and hardships endured by woman. Our silence, however, must not be set down either to indifference or to a want of independence. In our eyes, the rights of woman and the rights of man are identical—We ask no rights, we advocate no rights for ourselves, which we would not ask and advocate for woman. Whatever may be said as to a division of duties and avocations, the rights of man and the rights of woman are one and inseparable, and stand upon the same indestructible basis. If, for the well-being and happiness of man, it is necessary that he should hold property, have a voice in making the laws which he is expected to obey, be stimulatd by his participation in government to cultivate his mental faculties, with a view to an honorable fulfillment of his social obligations, precisely the same may be said of woman.

We advocate woman's rights, not because she is an angel, but because she is a woman, having the same wants, and being exposed to the same evils as man.

Whatever is necessary to protect him, is necessary to protect her. Holding these views, and being profoundly desirous that they should universally prevail, we rejoice at every indication of progress in their dissemination.

*Frederick Douglass' Paper*, October 30, 1851

## THE NATIONAL WOMAN'S RIGHTS CONVENTION AT SYRACUSE

We have been long familiar with public assemblies, and have never known one conducted so well. Whoever attended the Convention must be assured of the capabilities of woman to govern great assemblies amidst discordant elements. We will not attempt to give the speeches and resolutions. They are to be given to the public through the press, and a most valuable book they will make.

The resolutions were nobly expressive of woman's rights and wrongs, and a determination to bring the world to acknowledge the one and redress the other. The speeches were all of them of the first order. They showed the speakers to be deep thinkers, and well stored with the truths of philosophy and history, and eminently gifted with powers of eloquence. . . .

We have only to say, that this glorious Convention has done much good, not in regard to woman's rights only, but in regard to all human rights. It was a Convention of reformers of every description. When woman comes to have her rights, we have great reason to believe the reign of universal righteousness will have arrived. It is well said by some one, "as woman was the first, so will she be the last slave." May God speed the day of universal emancipation!

*Frederick Douglass' Paper*, September 17, 1852

## WOMEN AND POLITICS—THE NEXT PRESIDENCY, &C.

Women are beginning to have much influence in politics. There are few papers exerting greater influence than the *Saturday Visiter*, edited by Mrs. Swisshelm,[3] and the *Brattleboro Democrat*, edited by Mrs. Nichols,[4] both of them Free Democracy papers of great force and high intellectual order. Mrs. Swisshelm is less cautious and more impulsive, and springs at her purpose as if by instinct, and illustrates her position by the fervor of her enthusiasm, and jewels of rhetoric which come up from the exhaustless deep of her imagination to encompass it. Mrs. N., more cautious and less impulsive, takes more considerate aim, and is more sure of her mark, though not less effective in the general conflict.

It is quite an advance stage of political progress when women by the press and personal influence are forming public opinion for candidates to the highest offices in the gifts of the people. Ten years ago, should a woman presume to nominate candidates for the Presidency and Vice Presidency, their nominations would be both moral and ridiculous. But the fashions of this world pass away, and Mrs. Swisshelm brings forward her candidates for the Presidency, and presses their claims with as much propriety and ability as any statesman or politician of the day. Indeed, she is the first to bring her candidates into the field.

The only fault we find with her in this regard, is that she commits herself too early in the premises; and more, we hope we shall not be understood to complain, or be in any manner accusative. It is her right, and we would by no means interrupt it.

*Frederick Douglass' Paper*, February 25, 1853

## ANTOINETTE L. BROWN[5]

This Lady attended and addressed the Liberty Party Convention held at Syracuse.[6] She is one of the few women who contend for woman's right to vote, with rigid and beautiful consistency. She is a member of the Liberty Party, gives it the aid of her presence and counsel, serves on its committee, and really means what she says, when she demands the right to vote. With her the right to vote is no abstraction, a right to be asserted not exercised; she means voting, and we confess, our inability to see any reason in favor of man's right to choose his law-makers that does not equally apply to the case of women. Her right rests on the same foundation with his, and is in no respect inferior to his. The calmness, serenity, earnestness, ability and dignity with which Miss Brown advocates this right, compels the serious and respectful attention of all whom she addresses on the subject. We hope yet to hear her voice before an audience in Rochester, and that too on the platform of Corinthian Hall.

We understand that Miss Brown, is about to take charge of a congregation in the city of Troy, where she will preach regularly for some time to come. Why should the great lessons of Christianity not be taught as well by woman as man? Let cavillers answer.

*Frederick Douglass' Paper*, March 4, 1853

## WOMAN AND HER WISHES

An Essay inscribed to the Massachusetts Constitutional Convention, by Thomas Wentworth Higginson,[7] minister of the Worcester Free Church. Boston, Robert Wollcut, 21 Cornhill.

This pamphlet of twenty-six pages, is about the most racy and readable of anything on the subject of "woman's sphere," which has yet come under our observation. Fact and argument are here so airily and nicely blended, and important points so lucidly and rapidly presented, that to read it is like experiencing a drive over a smooth road, by the side of a crystal stream, changing in beauty as cloud or sun-light shades or brightens the winding surface. Men may laugh at the author—be indignant at the arrogance; they may vote themselves disgusted with this whole woman question; but that question is one which must be met, and that a time not far hence. Moreover, men will be compelled either to admit that the principles upon which they maintain their right to vote are utterly worthless or false, or they must admit that those principles apply as well to the rights of woman, as to the rights of man.

*Frederick Douglass' Paper,* March 11, 1853

## SOME THOUGHTS ON WOMAN'S RIGHTS

Woman has been the subject most prominent in the public discussions of our city during the past week, beginning with the meetings of the "Women's New York State Temperance Society" on Wednesday morning, and ending in Corinthian Hall on Sunday evening, when a large audience were addressed by Mr. William H. Channing,[8] and Miss Lucy Stone.[9] The wrongs, hardships, and inequalities, moral, mental, social, civil, and political, endured by woman, were forcibly and eloquently brought forward, and doubtless made a deep impression. No man could listen to Miss Stone's address on Sunday evening, without feeling that there was much reason in her speech, and in no part of it more than in that she portrayed the perfect dearth of motive and object afforded by society to young ladies. It was shown that on leaving school, about the most which is expected of a young lady, is that she will go home and "do little pretty things to wear"—nothing more.

This is all wrong; a woman should have every honorable motive to exertion which is enjoyed by man, to the full extent of her capacities and endowments. The case is too plain for argument. Nature has given woman the same powers, and subjected her to the same earth, breathes the same air, subsists on the same food, physical, moral, mental and spiritual. She has, therefore, an equal right with man, in all efforts to obtain and maintain a perfect existence. Speaking on this subject, and the demand which woman makes upon her brothers at this time, we cannot do better than quote from *The Una,*[10] for June, which has just come to hand. The editor says, (speaking of woman:)

"With her life all smothered on one side, it was but natural that it should be exaggerated on the other; and it was just as natural she should be compensated for being cruelly overruled, by being foolishly over-praised.—Women are not better, judged by a just and generous standard, than men. If the virgin was a woman, her divine son was a man.—This more than justice, habitually accorded to her moral nature, is but the cover for that greatly less than justice, which she has suffered in judgment and treatment at the hands of men. We ask for her less flattery, less adulation and more equity, fewer compliments and more completeness—fewer fair words and more fair treatment. We ask equal opportunity for free development, equal access to advantageous positions, equal wages for equal work, and equal rights for equal capacities. We cannot live upon incense, and he would not live upon alms. We are unwilling to be worshipped, for well we know that in the world's religion it means turning us out of the earth, under pretense of sending us to heaven. We are the abolitionists of slavery among women, and demand emancipation on the soil, not colonization in the clouds."

Well and happily said, every word of it—Woman should have justice as well as praise; and if she is to dispense with either, she can better afford to part with the latter than the former. It may be that there is something in our position, in this country—something in the injustice of which we are the subjects—something in the hatred of slavery and proscription, either natural or acquired by the hard circumstances of our early life—at any rate, from some cause—this whole woman question is exceedingly plain and simple, and commends itself at once to our mind. Woman, however, like the colored man, will never be taken by her brother and lifted to a position. What she desires, she must fight for. With her as with us, "Who would be free themselves must strike the blow." The price demanded for the good sought, is labor, self-sacrifice, the loss of popularity, loss of the good opinions of men. It is only when the object shall, in estimation, transcend all these that the effort will be commensurated with the conditions of success.

Does woman think she can build a house, and that that is the best appropriation of her time and the best application of her strength and talents? We say, let her go at it, and let shame fall upon the man who would hinder by word or dead, the laudable undertaking. But we repeat woman must practically as well as theoretically, asssert her rights. She must *do*, as well as *be*. A Doctor Harriet K. Hunt,[41] a Reverend Antoinette L. Brown or a Mrs. Paulina Davis,[12] all actively exercising the rights for which they contend, are proof against a world's sophistry and a world's ridicule. It is only in the heat of battle that balls lose their terror. So far as employments are concerned, the coast is comparatively clear, and woman can manage the matter for herself. But not so in the matter of voting. Men must do the work here.—They must, like true men and true Democrats, batter down the thick walls erected against woman at the ballot box, and let taxation and representation go together.

*Frederick Douglass' Paper*, June 10, 1853

## WOMEN'S NEW YORK STATE TEMPERANCE SOCIETY

The annual meeting of the "Women's New York State Temperance Society," whose proceedings we have chronicled on our first page, must not be permitted to pass without a few remarks from us. There was that in its spirit and action which justly demands animadversion—while there was much also entitling it to commendation. With perfect impartiality we hope to do the one, and with no desire to win favor from any of the parties, we would bestow the other. The Women's New York State Temperance Society is little more than a year old. It is a new organization—the originators of which, gave as a reason for launching it into the sea of public sentiment, as one of the instrumentalities to be used for the removal of intemperance, that woman had been cramped and denied an equal share in the activities of other Temperance organizations; and that she was therefore unable to do what in her heart she felt she could and ought to do, as woman in the Temperance cause. This reason was a valid one. It was boldly avowed and promptly acted upon, and out of it this Society sprang up—a handful then—but now counting its numbers by thousands. During the past year it has been, perhaps, the most active Temperance body in the United States. The readers have only to look at its proceedings, to know that it is a body of much energy and activity.

The agents of this Society have visited, during the year, every city in the State, and many of the towns and villages, scattering Temperance documents, and pleading the cause of Temperance with all the eloquence of woman's heart and voice, as they have gone.

The theme of these women, naturally enough, has been the peculiar and terrible sufferings of woman from the traffic in intoxicating liquors, and the necessity for the "Maine Law"[13] as a remedy. The great subject has been urged home upon the hearts of the people in a manner striking and effective, by both ability and novelty in the advocates. Woman's form on the platform, and woman's voice sounding through lofty halls, solemnly demanding of the sovereign people protection from the ravages of the devouring fiery demon, was well calculated to startle public apathy, and revive an almost expiring interest. In the earnestness, pathos, power and beauty of their appeals, men almost forgot to question the propriety of their action. For much of its efficiency the Society has been indebted to its happily chosen President, Mrs. E. C. Stanton,[14] a lady of fine talents and of high social position. Mrs. Stanton, though a wise counsellor, is withal a brave one, and belongs to the advanced guard of reformatory movements.—She was evidently in advance of the Society, to whose existence and prosperity she has contributed so largely.

This last remark will explain, what otherwise, perhaps, could scarcely be understood, of the action of this Society in electing officers for the present year. It will be seen that early in the sessions of the recent meeting, a committee was appointed to revise the Constitution of the Society, in several particulars: and among them, that part of the Constitution which rendered men ineligible to office, in the Society. This part of the Constitution was thought to be inconsistent with the principle and spirit of the Society, and to place the Society in the same attitude towards the men, as that maintained by the "New York State Temperance Society," toward the women. Mrs. Stanton was willing to have the Constitution made consistent with the principle of human equality; and standing firmly by her, was Miss Susan B. Anthony,[15] an agent of the Society, whose executive ability has been immensely serviceable to the cause during the past year.—These ladies, and others, were anxious to put the Society in harmony with principle.—On the other hand, strange to say, Mrs. Bloomer, the world-renowned Mrs. Bloomer, whose name has been supposed to represent the most ultra ideas of the equality of the sexes, was for keeping the men out of office.

The discussion on this subject was very animated and very instructive, and it showed pretty clearly the unwillingness of women, not less than of men, to surrender power, once in possession. Mrs. Bloomer, Mrs. Vaughn, Miss Clark,[16] (the latter a woman of unusual energy,) were for having the offices of the Society filled exclusively by ladies; and the result showed too, that they would not only have them filled by ladies, but by ladies of "their own particular opinions." The arguments used by these inconsistent ladies, were somewhat after this fashion: Let men become eligible to office in the Society, and they will soon control the entire action of the Society. Allow the men to come in and they will vote the women out. The charm of the Society consists in its being a woman's Society, &c., all which sounded very strange to us indeed; and when added to this, it was asserted by these ladies that woman's rights ought not to be talked of on their platform, we were astonished; for, with this very question, that of woman's wrongs and rights comes up legitimately.—The very moment woman rises in public to protest against the blighting traffic in rum, just so soon is raised the question of woman's rights. In order to act this public part, she must first demonstrate her fitness to do so.—The fact that such arguments were brought forward showed pretty plainly that the ladies have yet to comprehend the demands of their own position. One lady, in defining what she considered the position of the Society, told us that the Society was not connected with any other ism but Temperance. Seeing the division of feeling as well as of opinion which would probably ensue from a vote on the question, the subject was laid upon the table for the future action of the Society.

This question thus disposed of, it did seem to those who had favored the change in the Constitution of the Society, that things would go on as they had done during the past year. But not so; there was a determination, carrying with it the evidence of deliberation, and much previous concert to vote Mrs. Stanton out of office and to vote Mrs. Vaughn into Mrs. Stanton's place. The petty ambition for office (with the caucusing tactics to compass objects) displayed on this occasion, would have been as amusing as it was extraordinary, but for its lamentable likeness to the political meetings of men. The joke was carried so far by the majority, as to have printed tickets in the hands of "masculine" ticket-venders, with the names of certain favorites upon them for the offices of the Society. The mark of the beast was too apparent in all this, not to excite disgust in the minds of all who had looked upon the Society simply as a means for doing good, and not as a means of promoting anybody to office, or depriving anybody of office.

We may, perhaps, attach too much importance to a matter of this sort, but we look at it with the eye of one deeply concerned for the usefulness of the Society; and while we would not complain of the hesitation of the majority to adopt what was manifestly the right ground, and were willing that time should be given for thought and experience to do their proper work, we cannot regard Society, either as just, courteous, or grateful.

It was interesting to observe that such ladies as Mrs. Nichols, Mrs. Stanton, Miss Brown, Miss Stone, Miss Anthony, and Miss Wright, all ladies of marked ability, ranged themselves on the side of principle, as against expedience. The fact that these ladies do not assent to the position of the Society, should, of itself, (one would think), lead the Society to a reconsideration of its action.

Those who have long contended for woman's equality, and who assert that with man she should take her place in all the philanthropic movements of the day, were not little humbled by the course pursued by Mrs. Bloomer, Mrs. Vaughn, and Miss Clark.—Their position was a painful admission that woman cannot act to advantage in benevolent movements, unless she is secured in the possession of office by previous arrangements. She dare not let her claims depend upon her fitness, in comparison with that of man. For the ladies named distinctly affirmed that if, in electing offices of the Society, the question should be determined by qualification—men would be, invariably, chosen to fill the offices of the Society, to the exclusion of women! What is this but saying that we, the women, hold on to office in the Society, although we know that the offices would be better filled by men? Of course, we do not admit that the apprehensions of these ladies are well founded; but it is not the less humiliating that a woman like Mrs. Bloomer should share them.

*Frederick Douglass' Paper*, June 10, 1853

## THE JUST AND EQUAL RIGHTS OF WOMEN

To the Men and Women of New York:

The "Woman's Rights" Movement is a practical one, demanding prompt and efficient action for the relief of oppressive wrongs; and, as the Conventions held for several years past, in different States, have answered their end of arousing earnest public attention, the time has come for calling upon the People to reform the evils from which women suffer, by their Representatives in Legislative Assemblies.

The wise and humane of all classes in society, however much they may differ upon speculative points as to Woman's Nature and Function, agree that there are actual abuses of women, tolerated by custom and authorized by law, which are condemned alike by the genius of Republican Institutions and the spirit of the Christian Religion. Conscience and common sense, then, unite to sanction their immediate redress. Thousands of the best men and women, in all our communities, are asking such questions as these:

1. Why should not Woman's work be paid for according to the "quality" of the work done, and not the sex of the worker?

2. How shall we open for Woman's energies new spheres of well-remunerated industry?

3. Why should not Wives, equally with Husbands, be entitled to their own earnings?

4. Why should not Widows, equally with Widowers, become by law the legal guardians, as they certainly are by nature the natural Guardians, of their own children?

5. On what just ground do the laws make a distinction between Man and Woman, in regard to the ownership of property, inheritance, and the administration of estates?

6. Why should Women, any more than Men, be taxed without representation?

7. Why may not Women claim to be tried by a jury of their peers, with exactly the same right as Men claim to be and actually are?

8. If Women need the protection of the laws, and are subject to the penalties of the laws equally with Men, why should they not have an equal influence in making the Laws, and appointing Legislatures, the Judiciary, and Executive?

And finally, if Governments,—according to our National Declaration of Independence,—"derive their just powers from the consent of the governed," why should Women, any more than Men be governed without their own consent; and why, therefore, is not Woman's right to Suffrage precisely equal to Man's!

For the end of finding out practical answers to these and similar questions, and making suitable arrangements to bring the existing "wrongs of Woman," in the State of New York, before the Legislature at its next session,—we, the undersigned, do urgently request the Men and Women of the Commonwealth to assemble in Convention, in this city of Rochester, on Wednesday, November 9th, and Thursday, December 1st, 1853.

(Signed) Frederick Douglass, Elizabeth Cady Stanton, Susan B. Anthony, etc.

*Frederick Douglass' Paper*, November 25, 1853

## WOMAN'S RIGHTS: CIRCULATE THE PETITIONS

The design of the Convention held last week in Rochester, was to bring the subject of Woman's legal and civil disabilities, in a dignified form, before the Legislature of New York.

Convinced, as the friends of the movement are, that inconsistency with the principle of republicanism, females equally with males, are entitled to Freedom, Representation and Suffrage; and, confident as they are that Woman's influence will be found to be as refining and elevating in public, as all experience proves it to be in private, they claim that *one half* of the people and citizens of New York should no longer be governed by the other half, without consent asked and given.

Encouraged by reforms already made in the barbarous usages of Common Law, by the statutes of New York, the advocates of Woman's just and equal rights demand that this work of reform be completed, until every vestige of *partiality* be removed. It is proposed, in a carefully prepared Address to specify the remaining legal disabilities, from which the women of this State yet suffer; and a hearing is asked before a Joint Committee of both Houses, specially empowered to revise and amend the statutes.

Now is this movement right in principle? Is it wise in policy?

Should the females of New York be placed on a level of equality with males before the law? If so, let us petition for this impartial justice to women.

In order to insure this equal justice should the females of New York, like the males, have a voice in appointing the law makers and the law administrators? If so, let us petition for Woman's Right to Suffrage.

Finally, what candid man will be opposed to a reference of the whole subject to the Representatives of New York, whom the Men of New York themselves elected. Let us then petition for a *hearing* before the Legislature.

One word more, as to the Petitions, given below. They are *two* in number; one for the JUST AND EQUAL RIGHTS OF WOMEN; one for WOMAN'S RIGHT TO SUFFRAGE. It is designed that they should be signed by men and women of *lawful age*—that is of twenty-one years and upward. The following directions are suggested:

1. Let persons, ready and willing, sign *each* of the petitions; but let not those who desire to secure Woman's Just and Equal Rights, hesitate to sign that petition, because they have doubts as to the right and expediency of Woman's voting. The petitions will be kept separate, and offered separately. All fair-minded persons, of both sexes, ought to sign the *first* petition. We trust that many thousands are prepared to sign the *second* also.

2. In obtaining signatures, let men sign in one column, and women in another parallel column.

3. Let the name of the town and county, together with the number of signatures, be distinctly entered on the Petitions before they are returned.

4. Let every person, man or woman, interested in this movement, instantly and energetically circulate the petitions in their respective neighborhoods. We must send in the name of every person in the State, who desires full justice to woman, so far as it is possible. Up then friends, and be doing, *today*.

5. Let no person sign either petition, but *once*. As many persons will circulate petitions in the same town and county, it is important to guard against this *possible abuse*.

6. Finally, let every petition be returned to Rochester, directed to the Secretary of the Convention, Susan B. Anthony, on the first of February, without fail.

PETITION FOR THE JUST AND EQUAL RIGHTS OF WOMEN

The Legislature of the State of New York have, by the Acts of 1848 and 1849, testified the purpose of the People of this State to place Married Women on an equality with Married Men in regard to the holding, and devising of real and personal property.

We, therefore, the undersigned petitioners, inhabitants of the State of New York, male and female, having attained the age of legal majority, believing that Women, alike married and single, do still suffer under many and grievous legal disabilities, do earnestly request the Senate and Assembly of the State of New York to appoint a Joint Committee of both houses, to revise the Statutes of New York, and to propose such amendments as will fully establish the legal equality of Women and Men; and do hereby ask a hearing before such Committee by our accredited Representatives.

### PETITION FOR WOMEN'S RIGHT TO SUFFRAGE

Whereas, according to the Declaration of our National Independence, Governments derive their just powers from the consent of the governed, we earnestly request the Legislature of New York to propose to the people of the State such amendments of the Constitution of the State as will secure to Females an equal right to the Elective Franchise with Males; and we hereby request a hearing before the Legislature by our accredited representatives.

*Frederick Douglass' Paper*, December 25, 1853

## LUCY STONE AT MUSICAL FUND HALL, PHILADELPHIA

We were not prepared to see Miss Stone called to account for anything, looking like an abandonment of the cause of the colored people, as was the case in our last week's number; though we know how hard it is for abolitionists to comply, in all cases, with the obvious demands of the principles they have espoused. Circumstances do often arise in this negro-hating age and land, which almost compel them to shut the door in the faces of their sable brothers and sisters, and leave them outside to the buffetings of their enemies. It is not easy for any white abolitionist to stand with, and to share the bitter cup commended to the lips of our outcast race. The wonder is that any are found able to stand this trial of their anti-slavery faith. To do this, the heart must be strong, the eye single, and the whole body full of light. Our friend, Lucy Stone, for whom we cherish sentiments of high esteem, to say nothing of gratitude, has had such a trial, and we wish we could say, she has come out of it with credit to herself and honor to her cause; but facts say otherwise, and so must we.

When, some years ago, the Hutchinson family,[17] noble and warm-hearted band, were tricked into singing for the amusement of that old offender against the claims of human brotherhood, now gone to his account; and when Samuel R. Ward allowed himself to call a meeting in Philadelphia,[18] with seats reserved for white persons; and when Miss Greenfield, alias the Black Swan, perpetrated the offense of singing to her delighted oppressors in various parts of the country[19]—while people of her own color were carefully excluded on account of their color, we did not hestitate to enter our humble protest against such wound-inflicting conduct. What we did in the cases alluded to, we shall do now—for it is not good to have respect to persons. The cause of human freedom requires impartiality in its advocates, and believing Miss Stone to have erred as to her duty in the premises, and to have inflicted a wound on the cause dear to her, perhaps, not less than to ourselves, it is proper we should say so. She has loved the cause of human brotherhood too truly, and served it too nobly, and rebuked departures from it too boldly, to take our criticism in an unfriendly spirit.

When she learned that colored people were to be excluded from her lecture at Musical Fund Hall, it is plain that Miss Stone should have felt herself excluded. The public were invited to attend her lecture; and when she found that to gratify a malignant prejudice, and to brand with inferiority, a people already heart-broken, a hateful proscription was to be observed; the course of duty was plain. As an abolitionist and an honorable woman, she should have said, that neither by word or deed, will I sanction this outrage. But it was too late. Ah! there is the mistake. It would not have been too late had the report of this wrong come to her ear while she was yet speaking. An opportunity would have even then been given her, to have dealt a blow for freedom, upon the hoary head of the monster prejudice, far more stunning and destructive than any which by speech or letter she can now give. Had she left the platform, saying, take your money at the door; I cannot lecture under such proscription, she would have won the respect of everyone whose respect is worth having.

It may be said that in that case Miss Stone would have broken her engagement with the public; that she had invited the public to hear a lecture, and then refused to give it.—The answer is, that the contract, as she understood it, was already broken. A portion of the public had, through no fault of hers, already been excluded, their rights and feelings trampled upon, and to remain and speak under the circumstances, was to that extent, to sanction the outrage. The responsibility of the deed ought to have been thrown wholly on the heads of the barbarous proprietors of the Musical Fund Hall, and the public left to settle the account with them. Had the victims of this proscription been white persons, with every facility for righting their own wrongs, the case would admit of some paliation; but the defencelessness and dejection of our people aggravates every insult offered to them. We are too few and too feeble to bear up under the neglect of our friends, though we can perchance stand the insults of our enemies.

We confess to having been somewhat distrubed for our friend Lucy Stone's abolitionism, when we read of her recent visit to the South, and the encomiums showered upon her by the same presses that advertise men and women for the market, like horses, sheep and swine. We could not understand how it was, that one adopting the motto of "no union with slaveholders," as she does, could all at once become such a prodigious favorite of slaveholders. There was ground for the belief that our friend had allowed her mind to become darkened, and her noble heart's convictions to be stifled; that for the purpose of her visit southward, she could conceal, or at any rate not make prominent her anti-slavery sentiments.

It seems to us that one outburst of her noble and womanly eloquence in favor of freedom, such as we have heard from her lips in Corinthian Hall, would have scattered the admiring multitudes that thronged to hear her, quicker than they assembled. But she did not go there to speak for the slave—only for woman. Granted. Still, to speak for woman in a slave State where woman is made merchandise of, sold for the basest of purposes, robbed of all that makes woman honorable, without specifying these abominations, is to preach about the exceeding sinfulness of sin, without defining what sin is. The question as to whether a man or woman can consistently withhold for any purpose his or her convictions on the subject of slavery, has been discussed at much length, and with much ability by the anti-slavery journals of the land, in connection with such names as Cox and Hoby, Kossuth and Father Mathew, to say nothing of the Irish transport, John Mitchel, and the free church deputation.[20]—Kossuth went South to plead for woman; and so far as we know, both pursued the same course, both practically acted on the doctrine of non-intervention. May it not be, that having come, so recently from the South, where she had to say to her anti-slavery principles, stand aside, while I deal out truth, less offensive than anti-slavery.—She was the less disposed to adhere to her principles at Musical Fund Hall.

But whatever may have been the cause, Miss Stone has failed to embrace a good opportunity for testifying against a most unnatural and brutal prejudice; and thus to vindicate the principles of freedom and humanity, by the advocacy of which she has won the esteem and admiration of the noble and good, wherever her name and her deeds are known. This failure, and the insults to which such gentlemen as Chas. L. Reason were subjected,[21] may seem light, and quite unimportant in the eyes of some abolitionists; but we who have to endure the cuffs of pro-slavery, can ill bear to be deserted by our friends.

*Frederick Douglass' Paper*, February 17, 1854

## LETTER FROM FRANCIS BARRY.
## BERLIN, ERIE CO., OHIO

BRO. DOUGLASS:—I have read your article in relation to Lucy Stone, and her course at Musical Fund Hall, and also Charles L. Reason's letter on the same subject. I heartily endorse every word, both of the article and the letter. Having thus unqualifiedly endorsed your doctrine, allow me to say a few words in regard to its application. For you are aware that you do not merely contend for certain action in certain cases, but that you assert a principle, that demands application throughout the whole sphere of our activities. First, let me say that the man or woman cannot be found who does make such application of it; and for this simple reason, there are none so infallible, so supremely wise and good, so discerning and so just, as to recognize and honor all their obligations. One man is awake to one truth, and one set of obligations, and another to another.

Now, what is the principle, upon which your whole argument is based? Manifestly this—that one truth must not be sacrificed for the benefit of another. TRUTH IS ONE. This great fact, this sublime and supremely important truth, most reformers (to say nothing of the "rest of mankind" have yet to learn. Lucy Stone lost sight of it, when she consented to speak in a hall from which colored people had been excluded.—She thought to build up one truth, while another, by her permission, was being trampled in the dust. Vain thought!

"But suppose ye that" Lucy Stone "is a sinner above other" reformers? "I tell you nay." Did you, my brother, ever take part in a meeting or convention, in which one class of community (the class who do not usually dress in "male costume") were not expected to take a part, from whose committees &c., they were carefully excluded? Did you ever speak in a church, on any subject, from which any other person wishing to speak on another subject would be excluded? I take it for granted that it is no worse to shut a man out of your house, than to admit him and then thrust a gag in his mouth! I presume you frequently lecture on anti-slavery in houses that would be closed against an avowed Infidel or Spiritualist. I do not know that you would do any of these things but if you would not, you are more consistent than a great many other very good men.

FRANCIS BARRY.
*Frederick Douglass' Paper,* March 17, 1854

## MR. BARRY'S LETTER

The letter from Mr. Barry, in another column of our present number, designed to show that Miss Stone's departure from anti-slavery principles, in consenting, as she did, in the exclusion of colored people from a lecture of her's recently delivered in "Musical Fund Hall," Philadelphia, was simply a common occurence, and was not more reprehensible than similar acts of our own, is a well intended effort, quite plausible, but it falls entirely of its object. The cases put by our respected friend are only similar in their seeming; neither by speaking on a platform from which a woman is excluded, nor by consenting to speak in a meeting house not open to an infidel, places us in a similar transgression with Miss Stone, or any other white abolitionist, who find it convenient on occasions to turn their backs on their sable clients. We do not wish to hold Miss Stone up as a sinner above all others—far from it—but we do wish, while every other anti-slavery paper, old organized and all, are silent to bear our testimony upon what we conceive to be a vital point.

"All truth is one." Simply as all truths harmonize with each other, and come from the same great fountain of eternal goodness. All truths, however, are not equally clear to the human understanding, and cannot be known with equal certainty. There are things about which men may differ in opinion, and still act together where they may happen to agree.

A man's creed or his no creed may or it may not unfit him for the office of a public teacher; but a man's color cannot unfit him to be a learner. The first part of this proposition admits of a difference of opinion; the second does not. The distinction here is that what is doubtful in one case, is plain in the other; and while we would take a radical and stringent position in regard to what is self-evidently wrong, we would tolerate and co-operate with men who differ from us on matters which admit of a difference of opinion. A church votes that Frederick Douglass may lecture in its house against slavery. The same church votes that some other man shall not so lecture, because in its opinion, his creed or his no creed unfits him to speak in its house; we hold that it would be no sacrifice of truth for Frederick Douglass to go into such a church and to speak for the slave, and leave these parties to settle the other question for themselves. In case malice or other unworthy motives entered into his exclusion, our course would be otherwise, and of this we should have to judge in the light of the facts.

Again we are asked, Have you not taken a public part in meetings, from which was excluded from their public activities?—We answer, yes. We spoke last spring at the meeting of the American and Foreign Anti-Slavery Society. Well, according to friend Barry, we are quite as blame-worthy as Miss Stone. Let us see if the cases are similar. We think they are not, but are as widely different as are good and evil.

Woman is not excluded with a view to her degradation, or out of a spirit of hate. Nobody will pretend that she is. On the contrary, a sentiment quite opposite to malice dictates her exclusion. It is an error, and one which is to be met with light and truth. Far otherwise is the case of the black man's exclusion from public halls. A malicious determination to degrade, is here self-evident. The very spirit of the pit is here manifest, and against which no rebuke is too stringent. We cannot go with the multitude in such a sin without being partakers with them. Whatever may be our duty in regard to taking part in meetings where women are not allowed to speak, and to vote, it is plain that an abolitionist cannot consistently yield so far to the unreasoning and unreasonable malignity which slams the door in the black man's face, as to go in, and leave him on the outside to insult and degradation. That we may not be misunderstood, we repeat that the difference of our action in the cases supposed, is, first, men and women may honestly and innocently differ as to the wisdom and propriety of woman's speaking in public; second, that woman is not excluded from the public platform in a spirit of hate. On the other hand, there can be no honest difference of opinion, as to the right of the colored man to hear a public lecture; and he is only excluded by merciless tyranny and a most wicked hate.

*Frederick Douglass' Paper*, March 17, 1854


## ADDRESS TO THE LEGISLATURE OF THE STATE OF NEW YORK, ADOPTED BY THE STATE WOMAN'S RIGHTS CONVENTION, HELD AT ALBANY, TUESDAY AND WEDNESDAY, FEBRUARY 14TH AND 15TH, 1854. PREPARED BY ELIZABETH CADY STANTON, OF SENECA FALLS, N.Y.

To all those who wish to understand the subject indicated in the title of this pamphlet, and who wish to act upon the question of Woman's Rights, in the light of an intelligent judgment, we commend this publication. We have never seen woman's wrongs more ably stated nor her rights more clearly and eloquently asserted. If we have any criticism at all, to make upon a document so excellent, it is the seeming assumption for woman, which it contains of superiority over negroes. "We are (says the address, speaking for white women) moral, virtuous, and intelligent, and in all respects quite equal to the proud white man himself; and yet by your laws, we are classed with idiots, lunatics, and negroes." With all deference, we do not like this classification. We are willing to allow and contend that woman has as good a right as we have to the exercise of suffrage, but we cannot grant even as a matter of rhetoric or argument, that she has a better. Then we don't like now-a-days to be classed with "idiots and lunatics," more than do our fair sisters. We speak of this, however, merely as a slight blemish on an address, which, as a whole, is an honor to the hand that penned it, and the body that adopted it.

*Frederick Douglass' Paper*, March 3, 1854

## LUCY STONE AND SENATOR DOUGLAS

Mrs. Lucy Stone—Dear Madam: Your kind letter of the 8th inst. wishing me to be present at a Convention of the ladies of the North-West, to be convened at Chicago on the 12th of September next, to devise measures for the promotion of the happiness, and protection of the interests and rights of the female sex, has just been laid before me. You are right, dear Madam, when you say that I take a deep interest in all that concerns the ladies of our great and glorious country. And I need not now, after so many years of faithful labor in the cause of Popular Sovereignty, assure you that you have, in your endeavors to obtain the liberty of governing yourselves in your own way, subject only to the Constitution of the United States, the full confidence of my undivided sympathy. I regret, dear Madam, that business of great importance will prevent me from being present at your Convention.

I have the honor to remain, &c.,

S.A. DOUGLASS.[22]

Mrs. Lucy Stone has too frequently compromised her anti-slavery principles by a feverish desire for prominence and popularity, to surprise us by any sudden extravagance which she may perpetrate in the pursuit of the bubble of fame. By this letter of Senator Douglas, which Mrs. Stone doubtless caused to be published, the public is made acquainted with the fact that Mrs. Lucy Stone did go the length of especially inviting Senator Douglas to be present at the recent Woman's Rights Convention, held in Chicago. This Convention, be it remembered, was professedly held for the purpose of devising measures for the protection of the rights and the interests of woman. The object, it will be seen, was highly philanthropic and good, one which should be sought only by defensible and creditable means. In inviting Mr. Douglas, (of course it was a mark of respect, as well as a stroke of policy,) Mrs. Stone in our judgment pursued a course altogether reprehensible. We have heard of nearly all sorts of toadyism—religious toadyism, political toadyism, social toadyism—but here we have a specimen of philanthropical toadyism, about as little entitled to respect as the most contemptible of all the great family of toadyisms. Until now it has been customary to extend special invitations for such distinguished occasions, to men known and distinguished for their hearty and unequivocal sympathy for the cause to be supported by such conventions, on the principle that birds of a feather should flock together. But Mrs. Stone and her associates—if she had any—sets at defiance this very natural principle of association, by inviting a man to her Woman's Rights platform who, during his whole career, political and social, notwithstanding his high sounding phrases about equal rights and popular sovereignty, has chiefly distinguished himself for his utter disregard of such rights, and for his subtle schemes to undermine and overthrow them.—Who, but Mrs. Lucy Stone could have ever dreamed of honoring with an invitation to the Woman's Rights pltform a man already notorious for holding women in bondage, and for defending the sovereign mob in any of our territories to buy and sell women on the auction block? Who, but Mrs. Lucy Stone could have suspected Mr. Douglas of any sympathy with any rights, except the right to enslave and imbrute men, women and children? A cause may be damaged in two ways, and it becomes the Reformer to look out sharply for the tendency to either. One is by evincing too little respect for the opinions of those who happen to differ from us, and the other is too little respect for those who agree with us. There is no better way in the world to bring a cause into contempt, than by manifesting an undue solicitude for the support and countenance of the simple weather-gages of popularity. It is notable that, during the past summer, a dead set has been made upon the pleasure seekers to all our watering places, as if pleasure seekers and politicians were the best possible material out of which to make Woman's Rights Reformers. But in making a dash at Douglas, Mrs. Stone has thrown all the watering places into the shade. The Little Giant would have been a greater acquisition than a whole car load of pleasure seekers at Saratoga. But that sturdy fish was not to be caught, even by so dainty a bait flung by the gentle hand of Mrs. Stone.

We hear much about the wrongs of married women, the wrongs of single women, and about the inadequate wages paid to women, and the deficient representation of woman in public life—about the wrongs perpetrated against her in excluding her from the pursuit of the most lucrative branches of trade; we admit it all, and lament it all, and yet we may ask: what are all those wrongs, how trifling, how as the small dust of the balance when compared with the stupendous and ghastly wrongs perpetrated upon the defenseless slave woman?  Other women suffer certain wrongs, but the wrongs peculiar to woman out of slavery, great and terrible as they are, are endured as well by the slave woman, who has also to bear the ten thousand wrongs of slavery in addition to those common wrongs of woman. It is hard to be underpaid for labor faithfully performed; it is harder still not to be paid for labor at all. It is hard that woman should be limited in her opportunities for education; it is harder still to be deprived of all means of education. It is hard for the widow only to receive the third part of the property of her deceased husband; it is harder still to be a chattel person to all intents and purposes.—It is hard only to enjoy a qualified right to one's children; but it is harder still for a woman to have no rights which white men are bound to respect.

One would think that the first business of American women, who after all are highly favored above their sisters in many other countries, would be to make war upon the numberless outrages against the dignity of woman in the condition of a slave, and that they would instinctively perceive and shudder at anything in the slightest degree tending to uphold or connive at the slave system. Yet we see Mrs. Lucy Stone, the apostle of Woman's Rights, flinging the network of her notes of invitation about the neck of Stephen A. Douglas, as notorious for his contempt for Woman's Rights as Brigham Young is for the number of his wives! Our country abounds in startling contradictions. They are entirely too much the order of the day to excite any decided feeling. Everywhere there is a great ado made over small things, things comparatively harmless, while great and terrible crimes on the part of influential men and influential ladies are winked at in silence or plated with popular praise. It would not be very marvelous if the dainty slaveholding ladies of the south, seeing that their brother Stephen has been invited to cooperate with Mrs. Lucy Stone, would take the hint and form Wo-

man's Rights societies to redress "their" injuries, with a special provision in their constitution, however, that each member should
enjoy the sovereign right to decide whether she should enslave her
black sisters. This would be popular sovereignty of the Douglas
order, and seems to be quite approved in him by Mrs. Lucy Stone.
But who is Lucy Stone, the lady who thus seeks the co-operation of the incorrigible slaveholder, Stephen A. Douglas? She is a
lady mainly indebted for her present eminence to the anti-slavery
cause, and to the advocates of that cause. She of all others should
be keenly sensitive to the demands of the anti-slavery principle, and
should have been as ready to send for the devil himself to attend her
Woman's Rights Convention as to send for Douglas. Yet, after all,
as we said at the beginning, we are not surprised at Lucy. She, who
could betray her black brothers and sisters in Philadelphia to the
foul spirit of prejudice and caste, she who could lecture in St. Louis
in favor of Women's Rights, without mentioning the rights of slave
women, could hardly be expected to remember the contempt she
was heaping on the anti-slavery cause by honoring that prince of
negro haters to a seat in her Woman's Rights Convention. Mr.
Douglas, in declining the invitation, seems to have judged better
than Mrs. Lucy Stone of his fitness for the position to which she
had invited him. He evidently saw the awkwardness of appearing
on a platform with such rude men as Wendell Phillips,[23] T. W. Higginson, and others, whose notions of human rights are not influenced or limited to any distinctions in the forms of colors of mankind.

*Douglass' Monthly*, October 1859


## THE VOTE: SPEECH OF
## FREDERICK DOUGLASS IN BOSTON,
## JANUARY 25, 1865


It may be asked, "Why do you [Negroes] want it?" Some men
have got along very well without it. Women have not this right."
Shall we justify one wrong by another? This is a sufficient answer.
Shall we at this moment justify the deprivation of the negro of the

right to vote because some one else is deprived of that privilege? I hold that women as well as men have the right to vote, (applause,) and my heart and my voice go with the movement to extend suffrage to woman. But that question rests upon another basis than that on which our right rests.

*The Liberator*, February 10, 1865

## A THOUGHT

If any man can give one reason, drawn from the nature and constitution of man, why he should have a voice in the selection of those who shape the policy and make the Laws of the Government under which he lives, which reason does not apply equally and as forcibly to Woman, I for one, shall like to hear that reason. To me, the sun in the heavens at noonday is not more visible than is the right of woman, equally with man, to participate in all that concerns human welfare, whether in the Family, in Reform Associations, Educational Institutions, in the Church or in the State. Until this Right is admitted, secured, and exercised, count me among the friends of the "Woman's Rights Movement."

*The Woman's Advocate*, vol. I, January 1866, p. 16

## EQUAL RIGHTS CONVENTION FOR NEW YORK STATE, ALBANY, NEW YORK, NOVEMBER 20, 1866

Elizabeth Cady Stanton, Frederick Douglass, the Hon. A. J. Colvin, Parker Pillsbury,[24] Lucy Stone, Henry B. Blackwell,[25] Charles Lenox Remond,[26] Frances E. W. Harper,[27] and other advocates of Equal Rights were present and participated in the discussion.

Lucy Stone came forward to preside and the following committee was appointed: On Business—Elizabeth C. Stanton, Susan B. Anthony, Frederick Douglass, Parker Pillsbury, Elizabeth Jones, Charles Lenox Remond.

Mrs. Anthony read the call, and paid elaborate compliments to two or three papers of the State that had noticed the Convention favorably, reading editorials from *The Independent* and other journals. She protested against the assumption of the Republican papers that the women will all vote the Republican ticket when they get the ballot. The right of suffrage has always been extended by the Democratic party. She also protested against the use of the word "Copperhead,"[28] and looked to the Democrats quite as much as to the Republicans for the ballot. The Woman's Rights movement, and their cause in Congress is indebted to James Brooks[29] for championship.

Frederick Douglass remonstrated against such a tribute being paid to the Democratic party, explained Brooks's advocacy of woman's rights as the trick of the enemy to assail and endanger the rights of black men. He did it to make a point against the liberal policy of the Republicans and to shame them out of their anti-Slavery principles. He (Douglass) desired harmony, but if this eulogizing of the Democracy and best owing encomiums on such men as James Brooks and Samuel Cox[30] are to be persisted in there would be trouble in our family. (Applause and merriment.). . . .

Mr. Douglass said he had sometimes marveled that when men conceived the idea of forming a government for the well-being and progress of society, they ever attempted the experiment without the cooperation of woman. It must have been in a paroxysm of vanity and self-importance that he concluded that he could inaugurate and construct a Government without her assistance. We do not construct a government because we are male or female, but because we are human, because we are moral beings, capable of being influenced in our conduct by hope and fear, because we are liable to sin. By every fact to which man can appeal as a justification of his own right to a ballot, a woman can also appeal with equal force. Ours is called the best Government on earth—a masterpiece of statesmanship; and when men would be recondite as well as patriotic they discourse learnedly of the admirable adjustments and balances. But it has its defects; one of them this movement comes to remedy. It is weak, not because it is a republican government, but because claiming to be republican it has within itself so many anti-republican elements. He feared that the Convention, while claiming to be an "Equal Rights" Convention was in danger of becoming *merely* a woman's rights convention. The women must take the negro by the hand. With them it is a desirable matter; with us it is important; a question of life and death. With us disfranchisement means New Orleans, it means Memphis, it means New York mobs.[31] It means being driven from the work-shops and the schools. In some ways the men are *compelled* to protect the women; they protect them from the motives both of politeness and affection; but my race is hated, and in proportion to the measure of the dislike is the necessity of defense before and in the law. Nowhere in the world can woman attain the elective franchise without lifting the negro with her. A higher and better element will be introduced into our politics whenever either is led to the ballot-box.

Mr. Douglass then instanced and answered some of the stock objections to woman's franchise. He did not see why a woman should be any less womanly after walking to the polls with her husband than after walking to the Post-Office or the church with him. He demanded the ballot for woman because she is a citizen, because she is subject to the laws, because she is taxed, and because, if she commits a crime, she must be arrested, tried, convicted and punished like any other criminal. If we admit woman to be a reasoning and responsible being, we admit the whole. Woman must be harmoniously educated, and nothing but the ballot will give her an adequate knowledge of politics. Then we shall have the light of her intellect and the benefit of her remarkable intuition in our public affairs. In matters of criticism he felt more confidence in a woman of good sense and taste than in any man. Let woman go to the polls and express her will and we shall have different men and measures than we have now.

Mr. Douglass dissented from Mr. Pillsbury's opinion that it was best to dispense with invective. He could say "Copperhead" yet; and if Mr. Pillsbury had become very loving all at once, he must have repented of his sins. Love and hate involved each other. He rejoiced at the assemblage to-day, meeting for a movement so radical as this, it is auspicious of triumph. The infant being rocked in the cradle to-day will ere long be a giant. He knew of no better thing to bequeath to the children of this generation, than the prospect of someday taking part in the Government under which they live. He concluded by saying he found great difficulty in applying any qualification to the right of suffrage beyond that of common humanity. He was opposed to any educational or property test. The only safety for republican institutions is to be found in the ballot when placed in the hands of all, without regard to color or sex.

*New York Tribune*, December 21, 1866

## MEMORIAL OF THE AMERICAN EQUAL RIGHTS ASSOCIATION TO THE CONGRESS OF THE UNITED STATES

The undersigned, Officers and Representatives of the American Equal Rights Association, respectfully but earnestly protest against any change in the Constitution of the United States, or legislation by Congress, which shall longer violate the principle of Republican government, by proscriptive distinctions in right of suffrage and citizenship, on account of color or sex.

Your Memorialists would respectfully represent, that neither the colored man's loyalty, bravery on the battlefield and general good conduct, nor woman's heroic devotion to liberty and her country, in peace and war, have yet availed to admit them to equal citizenship, even in this enlightened and republican nation.

We believe that humanity is one in all those intellectual, moral and spiritual attributes, out of which grow human responsibilities. The Scripture declaration is, "so God created man in his own image: male and female created he them." And all divine legislation throughout the realm of nature recognizes the perfect equality of the two conditions. For male and female are but different conditions.

Neither color nor sex is ever discharged from obedience to law, natural or moral; written or unwritten. The commands, thou shalt not steal, nor kill, nor commit adultery, know nothing of sex in their demands; nothing in their penalty. And hence we believe that all *human* legislation which is at variance with the divine code, is essentially unrighteous and unjust.

Woman and the colored man are taxed to support many literary and humane institutions, into which they never come, except in the poorly paid capacity of menial servants. Woman has been fined, whipped, branded with red-hot irons, imprisoned and hung; but when was a woman tried by a jury of her peers?

Though the nation declared from the beginning that "all just governments derive their powers from the consent of the governed," the consent of woman was never asked to a single statute, however nearly it affected her dearest womanly interests or happiness. In the despotisms of the old world, of ancient and modern times, woman, profligate, prostitute, weak, cruel, tyranical, or otherwise, from Semiramis and Messalina, to Catherine of Russia and Margaret of Anjax, have swayed, unchallenged, imperial sceptres; while in this republican and Christian land, in the nineteenth century, woman, intelligent, refined in every ennobling gift and grace, may not even vote on the appropriation of her own property, or the disposal and destiny of her own children. Literally she has no *rights* which man is bound to respect; and her civil privileges she holds only by sufferance. For the power that gave can take away, and of that power she is no part. In most of the States, these unjust distinctions apply to woman, and to the colored man alike.

Your Memorialists fully believe that the time has come when such injustice should cease.

Woman and the colored man are loyal, patriotic, property-holding, tax-paying, liberty-loving citizens; and we cannot believe that sex or complexion should be any ground for civil or political degradation.

In our government, one-half the citizens are disfranchised by their sex, and about one-eighth by the color of their skin; and thus a large majority have no voice in enacting or executing the laws they are taxed to support and compelled to obey, with the same fidelity as the more favored class, whose usurped prerogative it is to rule.

Against such outrages on the very name of republican freedom, your Memorialists do and must ever protest. And is not our protest pre-eminently as just against the tyranny of "taxation without representation" as was that thundered from Bunker Hill, when our revolutionary fathers fired the shot that shook the world?

And your Memorialists especially remember, at this time, that our country is still reeling under the shock of a terrible civil war, the legitimate result and righteous retribution of the vilest slave system ever suffered among men. And in restoring the foundations of our nationality, your Memorialists most respectfully and earnestly say that all discriminations on account of sex or race may be removed; and that our government may be republican in *fact* as well as *form:* a GOVERNMENT BY THE PEOPLE, AND THE WHOLE PEOPLE; FOR THE PEOPLE AND THE WHOLE PEOPLE.

In behalf of the American Equal Rights Association,

Lucretia Mott,[32] President
Theodore Tilton,[33] Frederick Douglass,
Elizabeth Cady Stanton, Vice-Presidents
Susan B. Anthony, Secretary

*National Anti-Slavery Standard,* December 22, 1866

## RESOLUTION ADOPTED AT FIRST ANNUAL MEETING, AMERICAN EQUAL RIGHTS ASSOCIATION, NEW YORK CITY, MAY 9-10, 1867

Resolved, That the ballot, alike to women and men, means bread, education, intelligence, self-protection, self-reliance and self-respect; to the daughter it means diversified employment and a fair day's wages for a fair day's work; to the wife it means the control of her own person, property and earnings; to the mother it means the equal guardianship of her children; to all it means colleges and professions, open, equal opportunities, skilled labor and intellectual development.

Resolved, That the intrigues and conspiracies, the revolutions and wars attending both the beginning and progress of even the most liberal and enlightened governments, all including constant and crushing taxations and every form of oppression, together with the general premature mortality among the nations, are strong reasons for at least an investigation of the causes of these evils, if not the application of the most radical and extreme remedies for their removal.

Resolved, That the Reverend Henry Ward Beecher, Elizabeth Cady Stanton, and Frederick Douglass, be appointed a Committee to represent the National Equal Rights Association at the Constitutional Convention to be held in this State.

Resolved, That it is the duty of the coming Convention to amend the second article of the Constitution, to secure the right of suffrage to women, and black men not worth $250, and thus establish a republican form of government in the State of New York.

*National Anti-Slavery Standard*, June 1, 1867


## PROCEEDINGS OF THE AMERICAN EQUAL RIGHTS ASSOCIATION CONVENTION IN COOPER INSTITUTE, NEW YORK, MAY 14, 1868

. . . Mrs. Stone presented two forms of petition to Congress; one to extend suffrage to women in the District of Columbia and the Territories, the other for the submission of a proposition for a 16th Amendment to prohibit the States from disfranchising citizens on account of sex. Frederick Douglass made an acceptable speech in favor of the petitions. . . .

Frederick Douglass deprecated the seeming assertion of Rev. O. B. Frothingham, that one good cause was in opposition to another. I champion the right of the negro to vote. It is with us a matter of life and death, and therefore can not be postponed. I have always championed woman's right to vote; but it will be seen that the present claim of the negro is one of the most *urgent* necessity. The assertion of the right of women to vote meets nothing but ridicule; there is no deep seated malignity in the hearts of the people against her; but name the right of the negro to vote, all hell is turned loose and the Ku-klux and Regulators hunt and slay the unoffending black man. The government of this country loves women. They are the sisters, mothers, wives and daughters of our rulers; but the negro is loathed. Women should not censure Mr. Phillips, Mr. Greeley,[35] or Mr. Tilton [for having urged the priority of the vote for the negro], all have spoken eloquently for woman's rights. We are all talking for woman's rights, and we should be just to all our friends and enemies. There is a difference between the Republican and Democratic parties.

OLYMPIA BROWN:[36] What is it?

FREDERICK DOUGLASS: The Democratic party has, during the whole war, been in sympathy with the rebellion, while the Republican party has supported the Government.

OLYMPIA BROWN: How is it now?

FREDERICK DOUGLASS: The Democratic opposes impeachment,[37] and desires a white man's government.

OLYMPIA BROWN: What is the difference in *principle* between the position of the Democratic party opposing the enfranchisement of 2,000,000 negro men, and the Republican party opposing the emancipation of 17,000,000 white women?

FREDERICK DOUGLASS: The Democratic party opposes suffrage to both; but the Republican party is in favor of enfranchising the negro and is largely in favor of enfranchising woman. Where is the Democrat who favors woman suffrage? (A Voice in the audience, "Train!"[38]) Yes, he hates the negro, and that is what stimulates him to substitute the cry of emancipation for women. The negro needs suffrage to protect his life and property, and to ensure him respect and education. He needs it for the safety of reconstruction and the salvation of the Union; for his own elevation from the position of a drudge to that of an influential member of society. If you want women to forget and forsake frivolity, and the negro to take pride in becoming a useful and respectable member of society, give them both the ballot.

OLYMPIA BROWN: Why did Republican Kansas vote down negro suffrage?[39]

FREDERICK DOUGLASS: Because of your ally, George Francis Train!

OLYMPIA BROWN: How about Minnesota without Train? The Republican party is a party and cares for nothing but party! It has repudiated both negro suffrage and woman suffrage.

FREDERICK DOUGLASS: Minnesota lacked only 1,200 votes of carrying suffrage. All the Democrats voted against it, while only a small portion of the Republicans did so. And this was substantially the same in Ohio and Connecticut. The Republican party is about to bring ten states into the Union; and Thaddeus Stevens[40] has reported a bill to admit seven, all on the fundamental basis of constitutions guaranteeing negro suffrage forever.[41]

OLYMPIA BROWN again insisted that the party was false, and that now was the time for every true patriot to demand that no new State should be admitted except on the basis of suffrage to women as well as negroes.

LUCY STONE controverted Mr. Douglass' statement that women were not persecuted for endeavoring to obtain their rights, and depicted in glowing colors the wrongs of women and the inadequacy of the laws to redress them. Mrs. Stone also charged the Republican party as false to principle unless it protected women as well as colored men in the exercise of their right to vote.

Elizabeth Cady Stanton, Susan B. Anthony, and
Mtilda Joslyn Gage, eds.

*History of Woman Suffrage* (New York, 1882), vol. II, pp. 310-312

## TO JOSEPHINE SOPHIE WHITE GRIFFING[42]
## ROCHESTER SEPT. 27, 1868

My dear Friend:

I am impelled by no lack of generosity in refusing to come to Washington to speak in behalf of woman's suffrage. The right of woman to vote is as sacred in my judgment as that of man, and I am quite willing at any time to hold up both hands in favor of this right. It does not however follow that I can come to Washington or go elsewhere to deliver lectures upon this special subject. I am now devoting myself to a cause not more sacred, certainly more urgent, because it is one of life and death to the long-enslaved people of this country, and this is: negro suffrage. While the negro is mobbed, beaten, shot, stabbed, hanged, burnt and is the target of all that is malignant in the North and all that is murderous in the South, his claims may be preferred by me without exposing in any wise myself to the imputation of narrowness or meanness toward the cause of woman. As you very well know, woman has a thousand ways to attach herself to the governing power of the land and already exerts an honorable influence on the course of legislation. She is the victim of abuses, to be sure, but it cannot be pretended I think that her cause is as urgent as that of ours. I never suspected you of sympathizing with Miss Anthony and Mrs. Stanton in their course. Their principle is: that no negro shall be enfranchised while woman is not. Now, considering that white men have been enfranchised always, and colored men have not, the conduct of these white women, whose husbands, fathers and brothers are voters, does not seem generous.

Very truly yours-
Fredk Douglass

*Griffing Papers,* Columbia University Library,
Rare Book Division, Special Collections

## PROCEEDINGS OF THE AMERICAN EQUAL RIGHTS ASSOCIATION CONVENTION, STEINWAY HALL, NEW YORK CITY, MAY 12, 1869

MR. DOUGLASS:[43] I come here more as a listener than to speak and I have listened with a great deal of pleasure to the eloquent address of the Rev. Mr. Frothingham and the splendid address of the President. There is no name greater than that of Elizabeth Cady Stanton in the matter of woman's rights and equal rights, but my sentiments are tinged a little against *The Revolution.* There was in the address to which I allude the employment of certain names, such as "Sambo,"

and the gardener, and the bootblack, and the daughters of Jefferson
and Washington and other daughters. (Laughter.) I must say that I
asked what difference there is between the daughters of Jefferson
and Washington and other daughters. (Laughter). I must say that I
do not see how any one can pretend that there is the same urgency
in giving the ballot to woman as to the negro. With us, the matter is
a question of life and death, at least, in fifteen States of the Union.
When women, because they are women, are hunted down through
the cities of New York and New Orleans; when they are dragged
from their houses and hung upon lamp-posts; when their children
are torn from their arms, and their brains dashed out upon the
pavement; when they are objects of insult and outrage at every turn;
when they are in danger of having their homes burnt down over
their heads; when their children are not allowed to enter schools;
then they will have an urgency to obtain the ballot equal to our
own. (Great applause.)

A VOICE:—Is that not all true about black women?

MR. DOUGLASS:—Yes, yes, yes; it is true of the black woman, but
not because she is a woman, but because she is black. (Applause).
Julia Ward Howe[44] at the conclusion of her great speech delivered
at the convention in Boston last year said: "I am willing that the
negro shall get the ballot before me." (Applause.) Woman! why,
she has 10,000 modes of grappling with her difficulties. I believe that
all the virtue of the world can take care of all the evil. I believe that
all the intelligence can take care of all the ignorance. (Applause.) I
am in favor of woman's suffrage in order that we shall have all the
virtue and vice confronted. Let me tell you that when there were
few houses in which the black man could have put his head, this
wooly head of mine found a refuge in the house of Mrs. Elizabeth
Cady Stanton, and if I had been blacker than sixteen midnights,
without a single star, it would have been the same. (Applause.)

MISS ANTHONY:—The old anti-slavery school says women must
stand back and wait until the negroes shall be recognized. But we
say, if you will not give the whole loaf of suffrage to the entire people, give it to the most intelligent first. (Applause.) If intelligence,
justice, and morality are to have precedence in the Government,
let the question of woman be brought up first and that of the negro
last. (Applause.)[45] While I was canvassing the State with petitions
and had them filled with names for our cause to the Legislature, a

man dared to say to me that the freedom of women was all a theory and not a practical thing. (Applause.) When Mr. Douglass mentioned the black man first and the woman last, if he had noticed he would have seen that it was the men that clapped and not the women. There is not the woman born who desires to eat the bread of dependence, no matter whether it be from the hand of father, husband, or brother; for any one who does so eat her bread places herself in the power of the person from whom she takes it. (Applause.) Mr. Douglass talks about the wrongs of the negro; but with all the outrages that he to-day suffers, he would not exchange his sex and take the place of Elizabeth Cady Stanton. (Laughter and applause.)

MR. DOUGLASS: I want to know if granting you the right of suffrage will change the nature of our sexes? (Great laughter.)

MISS ANTHONY: It will change the pecuniary position of woman; it will place her where she can earn her own bread. (Loud applause.) She will not then be driven to such employments only as man chooses for her.

MRS. NORTON said that Mr. Douglass' remarks left her to defend the Government from the inferred inability to grapple with the two questions at once. It legislates upon many questions at one and the same time, and it has the power to decide the woman question and the negro question at one and the same time. (Applause.)

MRS. LUCY STONE:—Mrs. Stanton will, of course, advocate the precedence for her sex, and Mr. Douglass will strive for the first position for his, and both are perhaps right. If it be true that the government derives its authority from the consent of the governed, we are safe in trusting that principle to the uttermost. If one has a right to say that you can not read and therefore can not vote, then it may be said that you are a woman and therefore cannot vote. We are lost if we turn away from the middle principle and argue for one class. . . . The gentleman who addressed you claimed that the negroes had the first right to the suffrage, and drew a picture which only his great word-power can do. He again in Massachusetts, when it had cast a majority in favor of Grant and negro suffrage, stood upon the platform and said that woman had better wait for the negro; that is, that both could not be carried, and that the negro had better be the one. But I freely forgave him because he felt as he spoke. But woman suffrage is more imperative than his own; and I want to remind the audience that when he says what the Ku-Kluxes[46]

did all over the South, the Ku-Kluxes here in the North in the shape
of men, take away the children from the mother, and separate them
as completely as if done on the block of the auctioneer. Over in
New Jersey they have a law which says that *any* father—he might
be the most brutal man that ever existed—*any* father, it says, whether
he be under age or not, may by his last will and testament dispose
of the custody of his child, born or to be born, and that such disposition shall be good against all persons, and that the mother may
not recover her child; and that law modified in form exists over
every State in the Union except in Kansas. Woman has an ocean of
wrongs too deep for any plummet, and the negro, too, has an ocean
of wrongs that can not be fathomed. There are two great oceans;
in the one is the black man, and in the other is the woman. But I
thank God for that XV. Amendment, and hope it will be adopted
in every State. I will be thankful in my soul if *any* body can get
out of the terrible pit. But I believe that the safety of the government
would be more promoted by the admission of woman as an element of restoration and harmony than the negro. I believe that the
influence of woman will save the country before every other power.
(Applause.) I see the signs of times pointing to this consummation,
and I believe that in some parts of the country women will vote for
the President of the United States in 1872. . . .

MRS. PAULINE W. DAVIS said she would not be altogether satisfied
to have the XVth Amendment passed without the XVIth, for woman
would have a race of tyrants raised above her in the South, and the
black women of that country would also receive worse treatment
than if the Amendment was not passed. Take any class that have
been slaves, and you will find that they are the worst when free,
and become the hardest masters. The colored women of the South
say they do not want to get married to the negro, as their husbands
can take their children away from them, and also appropriate their
earnings. The black women are more intelligent than the men, because they have learned something from their mistresses. She then
related incidents showing how black men whip and abuse their
wives in the South. One of her sister's servants whipped his wife
every Sunday regularly. (Laughter.) She thought that sort of men
should not have the making of the laws for the government of the
women throughout the land. (Applause.)

MR. DOUGLASS said that all disinterested spectators would con-

cede that this Equal Rights meeting had been pre-eminently a Woman's Rights meeting. (Applause.) They had just heard an argument
with which he could not agree—that the suffrage to the black men
should be postponed to that of the women. . . . "I do not believe the
story that the slaves who are enfranchised become the worst of
tyrants. (A voice, "Neither do I." Applause.) I know how this theory
came about. When a slave was made a driver, he made himself
more officious than the white driver, so that his master might not
suspect that he was favoring those under him. But we do not intend
to have any master over us. (Applause.)"

THE PRESIDENT (MRS. STANTON) argued that not another man should
be enfranchised until enough women are admitted to the polls to
outweigh those already there. (Applause.) She did not believe in
allowing ignorant negroes and foreigners to make laws for her to
obey. (Applause.)

MRS. HARPER (colored) said that when it was a question of race,
she let the lesser question of sex go. But the white women all go for
sex, letting race occupy a minor position. She liked the idea of work-
women, but she would like to know if it was broad enough to take
colored women.

MISS ANTHONY and several others: Yes, yes.

MRS. HARPER said that when she was at Boston there were sixty
women who left work because one colored woman went to gain a
livelihood in their midst. (Applause.) If the nation could only handle
one question, she would not have the black woman put a single
straw in the way, if only the men of the race could obtain what
they wanted. (Great applause.). . .

Stanton, Anthony, and Gage, eds.
*History of Woman Suffrage*, vol. II, pp. 382-384, 391-392.[46]

## THE WOMAN QUESTION

Articles on the duty of women have grown in journals, opposing
her enfranchisement. Have her well-wishers so called got discouraged,
or are they in a state of despair at her inability to comprehend her
proper sphere, or is it that they are in a state of rumination how
best to benefit her?

It must be hard to have such grave and earnest appeals as those
made by the male conservatives misunderstood. Women were

urged to give up the frivolities of fashion, and cultivate their mind—become a companion to man and not be a butterfly. In answer to this appeal many toned down their dress, and took no more pains to be beautiful, depending upon their literary attainments to charm withall. But the "Bas Bleu," or the blue stocking horrified their well wishers, and the butterfly continued to be petted. Then the reformers ascertained that it was not the graces of the toilet that they wished to banish, and allow that woman to be acceptable, must attract by paying attention to ornament. But she must enlarge her mind, become acquainted with current topics, be interested in what interests man, and so be prepared to counsel him and instruct the youth. This advice too has been heeded. Women fully alive to the questions and duties of the hour have appeared. They come arrayed in tasteful garments, with well kept hair, full of grace, attracting not only by their elegance in dress and manner, but by their knowledge of outside as well as home affairs. They bring with them the same considerations to public matters, that they give to household wants; after making themselves mistress of the state of the case, they ask what is my duty in the premises, and how can I remedy existing evils? Full of zeal they come forward to assist man in his arduous duties; and thus prove what mistaken, misguided creatures they are.

Yet we think that the woman's suffrage movement has gained too much to recede, though it has lost much by its recent defeat in Massachusetts.[47] It is advocated among our great and good men, which will render it impossible for old fogies to shelve it, or for intemperate advocates to defeat it by a mistaken zeal!

The reform is no longer confined to the few earnest women who, for the last twenty years, have beset every Legislature with their petitions, and addressed those honorable bodies, and the public generally, to convince them that they were "not mad, but set forth the words of truth and soberness." And much has been gained to render possible an easy solution of the problem as to what is woman's proper sphere.

Her zeal and assurance have been so great that she is already gaining freedom of choice, and making circumstances yield to her energy, sagacity, and experience. She now seeks only the opportunity to prepare herself for the position she would occupy. Already the aspirations of women have led them to prove, by exertion, that they could fill with credit and success places which before it was considered could only be filled by men. The effect has been to ennoble those employments which have always been considered as solely within the province of womanhood.

Working women's clubs are being organized, and working women are pleading their own cause that their wrongs may be known and redressed. Thus the "Song of the Shirt" loses much of its woe. Domestic duties are being reduced to a science, or will be handed over to co-operative societies, and so hopeful are the signs that one of our great writers says she would ask no better fortune for her sister, should she be left destitute, than a place in the house of some well-regulated family. May not public opinion become so rational that domestic service will be regarded as being respectable enough for one to enter upon its duties without losing caste, and accede to the occupancy of any high positions assumed by woman without some man regarding her as his probable victim?

Now that the fifteenth amendment is a finality, and the colored man has become so important a member of the body-politic, let the colored women be prepared when the sixteenth amendment becomes law to co-operate in the various schemes which will be presented to their favor.

*The New Era*, May 12, 1870

## WOMAN SUFFRAGE MOVEMENT

The simplest truths often meet the sternest resistance, and are slowest in getting general acceptance. There are none so blind as those who will not see, is an old proverb. Usage and prejudice, like forts built of sand, often defy the power of shot and shell, and play havoc with their besiegers. No simpler proposition, no truth more self-evident or more native to the human soul, was ever presented to human reason or consciousness than was that which formed our late anti-slavery movement. It only affirmed that every man is, and of right ought to be, the owner of his own body; and that no man can rightfully claim another man as his property. And yet what a tempest and whirlwind of human wrath, what clouds of ethical and theological dust, this simple proposition created. Families, churches, societies, parties, and States were riven by it, and at last the sword was called in to decide the questions which it raised. What was true of this simple truth was also true as to the people's right to a voice in their own Government, and the right of each man to form for himself his own religious opinions. All Europe ran blood before humanity and reason won this sacred right from priestcraft, bigotry, and superstition. What to-day seems simple, obvious, and undeniable, men looking through old customs, usages, and prejudices in other days denied altogether. Our friends of the woman's suffrage movement should bear this fact in mind, and share the patience of truth while they advocate the truth. It is painful to encounter stupidity as well as malice; but such is the fate of all who attempt to reform an abuse, to urge on humanity to nobler heights, and illumine the world with a new truth.

Now we know of no truth more easily made appreciable to human thought than the right of woman to vote, or, in other words, to have a voice in the Government under which she lives and to which she owes allegiance. The very admission that woman owes allegiance, implies her right to vote. No man or woman who is not consulted can contract as obligation, or have an obligation created for him or her as the case may be. We can owe nothing by the mere act of another. Woman is not a consenting party to this Government. She has never been consulted. Ours is a Government of men, by men, each agreeing with all and all agreeing with each in respect to certain fundamental propositions, and women are wholly excluded. So far as respects its relation to woman, our Government is in its essence, a simple usurpation, a Government of force, and not of reason. We legislate for woman, and protect her, precisely as we legislate for and protect animals, asking the consent of neither.

It is nothing against this conclusion that our legislation has for the most part been eminently just and humane. A despotism is no less a despotism because the reigning despot may be a wise and good man. The principle is unaffected by the character of the man who for the moment may represent it. He may be kind or cruel, benevolent or selfish, in any case he rules according to his own sovereign will— and precisely such is the theoretical relation of our American Government toward woman. It simply takes her money without asking her consent and spends the same without in any wise consulting her wishes. It tells her that there is a code of laws which men have made, and which she must obey or she must suffer the consequences. She is absolutely in the hands of her political masters: and though these may be kind and tender hearted, (the same was true of individual slave masters, as before stated,) this in nowise mitigates the harshness of the principle—and it is against this principle we understand the woman's suffrage movement to be directed. It is intended to claim for woman a place by the side of man, not to rule over him, not to antagonize him, but to rule with him, as an equal subject to the solemn requirements of reason and law.

To ourselves the great truth underlying this woman's movement is just as simple, obvious, and indisputable as either of the great truths referred to at the beginning of this article. It is a part of the same system of truths. Its sources are individuality, rationality, and sense of accountability.

If woman is admitted to be a moral and intellectual being, possessing a sense of good and evil, and a power of choice between them, her case is already half gained. Our natural powers are the foundation of our natural rights; and it is a consciousness of powers which suggests the exercise of rights. Man can only exercise the powers he possesses, and he can only conceive of rights in presence of powers. The fact that woman has the power to say "I choose this" rather than "that" is all-sufficient proof that there is no natural reason against the exercise of that power. The power that makes her a moral and an accountable being gives her a natural right to choose the legislators who are to frame the laws under which she is to live, and the requirements of which she is bound to obey. By every fact and by every argument which man can wield in defence of his natural right to participate in government, the right of woman so to participate is equally defended and rendered unassailable.

Thus far all is clear and entirely consistent. Woman's natural abilities and possibilities, not less than man's, constitute the measure of her rights in all directions and relations, including her right to participate in shaping the policy and controlling the action of the Government under which she lives, and to which she is assumed to owe obedience. Unless it can be shown that woman is morally, physically, and intellectually incapable of performing the act of voting, there can be no natural prohibition of such action on her part. Usage, custom, and deeply rooted prejudices are against woman's freedom. They have been against man's freedom, national freedom, religious freedom, but these will all subside in the case of woman as well as elsewhere. The thought has already been conceived; the word has been spoken; the debate has begun; earnest men and women are choosing sides. Error may be safely tolerated while truth is left free to combat it, and nobody need fear the result. The truth can hurt nothing which ought not to be hurt, and it alone can make men and women free.

*The New National Era,* October 20, 1870

## WOMAN AND THE BALLOT

In the number preceding the present the natural right of woman to a voice in the Government under which she lives and to which she is assumed to owe allegiance, and for the support of which she is compelled like male citizens to pay taxes, was briefly discussed. It is proposed now to adduce some reasons resting on other facts why woman should be allowed to exercise her indisputable natural right to participate in government through the same channels and instrumentalities employed by men. That society has a right to employ for its preservation and success all the mental, moral, and physical power it thus possesses and can make available, is a truth requiring no argument to make it clear. Not less clear is it, at least to some minds, that society, through its forms of government, ought to exercise that right. It has many rights and duties; but the right and duty to cripple and maim itself, or to deprive itself of any power it naturally possesses, are not among them. A man may cut off his arms and feet, pluck out his eyes, and society may deprive itself of its natural powers for guidance and well-being, but enlightened reason assents neither to the action of the one nor of the other. In this respect nations and individuals stand upon the same footing. The highest good is the supreme law for both, and each after his kind must bear the penalty attached to transgression. The Chinese woman may cripple her feet in obedience to custom, and the Hindoo woman throw herself in the consuming flame for superstition, but nature's laws exact their full measure of pain from whatever motive or through whatever motive or through whatever ignorance her mandates are violated.

The grand idea of American liberty is coupled with that of universal suffrage; and universal suffrage is suggested and asserted by universal intelligence. Without the latter the former falls to the ground; and unless suffrage is made co-extensive with intelligence something of the natural power of society essential to its guidance and well-being is lost. To deny that woman is capable of forming an intelligent judgment concerning public men and public measures, equally with men, does not meet the case; for, even if it were granted, the fact remains the same that woman, equally with men, possesses such intelligence; and that such as it is, and because it is such as it is, woman, in her own proper person has a right for herself to make it effective. To deprive her of this right is to deprive her of a part of her natural dignity, and the State of a part of its mental power of direction, prosperity, and safety; and thus a double wrong is perpetuated.

Man in his arrogance has hitherto felt himself fully equal to the work of governing the world without the help of woman. He has kept the reins of power securely in his hands, and the history of nations and the present experience of the world show the woeful work he has made of governing. He has made human history a history of war and blood even until now. The world to-day seems as fierce, savage, and bloody as a thousand years ago, and there is not one of all the civilized nations of the earth which has not mortgaged the energies of unborn generations to pay debts contracted by the crimes and blunders of its Government. Whether the case would have been different had woman's voice been allowed in national affairs, admits of little debate. War is among the greatest calamities incident to the lives of nations. They arrest the progress of civilization, corrupt the sources of morality, destroy all proper sense of the sacredness of human life, perpetuate the national hate, and weigh down the necks of after coming generations with the burdens of debt. To nothing more than to war is woman more instinctively opposed. If the voices of wives, sisters, and mothers could be heard no standing armies would menace the peace of the world to-day, and France and Prussia would not be bathing their hands in each other's warm blood.[48] Napoleon told us the "Empire means peace," and we say that Republics mean peace, but neither Empires, Republis, nor Monarchies can mean peace while men alone control them. The vote of women is essential to the peace of the world. Her hand and voice naturally rises against the shedding of human blood. Against this conclusion cases may be cited, but they are exceptional and abnormal. Woman as woman, far more than man as man, is for peace. That slavery imparted something of its own blood-thirsty spirit to the women of the South—that superstition and fanaticism have led some women to consent to the slaughter of their children and to the destruction of themselves—cannot be taken against the natural gentleness and forbearance of the sex as a whole. She naturally shudders at the thought of subjecting her loved ones to the perils and horrors of war, and her vote would be a peace guaranty to the world. While society consents to exclude women from all participation in the guidance of its Government, it must consent to standing armies, preparations for war calculated to bring them on, and smite itself into blood and death.

But whatever may be thought as to the consequences of allowing women to vote, it is plain that women themselves are divested of a large measure of their natural dignity by their exclusion from such participation in Government. Power is the highest object of human respect. Wisdom, virtue, and all great moral qualities command respect only as powers. Knowledge and wealth are nought but powers. Take from money its purchasing power, and it ceases to be the same object of respect. We pity the impotent and respect the powerful everywhere. To deny woman her vote is to abridge her natural and social power, and deprive her of a certain measure of respect. Everybody knows that a woman's opinion of any lawmaker would command a larger measure of attention had she the means of making opinion effective at the ballot-box. We despise the weak and respect the strong. Such is human nature. Woman herself loses in her own estimation by her enforced exclusion from the elective franchise just as slaves doubted their own fitness for freedom, from the fact of being looked upon as only fit for slaves. While, of course, woman has not fallen so low as the slave in the scale of being, (her education and her natural relation to the ruling power rendering such degradation impossible,) it is plain that, with the ballot in her hand, she will ascend a higher elevation in her own thoughts, and even in the thoughts of men, than without that symbol of power. She has power now—mental and moral power— but they are fettered. Nobody is afraid of a chained lion or an empty gun.

It may be said that woman does already exercise political power— that she does this through her husband, her father and others related to her, and hence there is no necessity for extending suffrage to her, and allowing her to hold office. This objection to the extension of suffrage, is true in the same sense, that every disfranchised people, esepecially if intelligent, must exert some influence and compel a certain degree of consideration among governing classes, but it is no conclusive argument. If a man is represented in part by another, there is no reason in that why he may not represent himself as a whole, or if he is represented by another, there is no reason in that why he may not represent himself—and the same is true of woman. The claim is that she is represented by man, and that she does therefore indirectly participate in Government. Suppose she does, and the question at once comes if it be right for woman to participate in government indirectly how can it be wrong for her to do so directly? That which is right in itself, is equally right whether done by the principal or the agent especially if equally well done. So far as ability to perform the mere act of voting is concerned woman is as well qualified to do that as to drop a letter in the post office, or to receive one at the window. Let her represent herself. This is the simplest and surest mode of representation. The old slaveholders used to represent the slaves, the rich landowners of other countries represent the poor, and the men in our country claim to represent woman, but the true doctrine of American liberty plainly is, that each class and each individual of a class should be allowed to represent himself—that taxation and representation should go together. Woman having intelligence, capable of an intelligent preference for the kind of men who shall make the laws under which she is to live, her natural dignity and self-respect coupled with the full enjoyment of all her rights as a citizen, her welfare and happiness equally the objects of solicitude to her as to others, affected as deeply by the errors, blunders, mistakes and crimes committed by the Government, as any part of society, especially suffering from the evils of war, drunkenness and immoralities of every kind, instinctively gentle, tender, peaceful, and orderly. She needs the ballot for her own protection, and men as well as women need its concession to her for the protection of the whole. Long deprived of the ballot, long branded as an inferior race—long reputed as incapable of exercising the elective franchise, and only recently lifted into the privileges of complete American citizenship, we cannot join with those who would refuse the ballot to women or to any others of mature age and proper residence, who bear the burdens of the Government and are obedient to the laws.

*The New National Era,* October 27, 1870

## A UNION OF HEARTS[49]

Among the friends of woman's enfranchisement there has been manifested for many months past a feeling that if the two existing national organizations for this object could be merged into one, having one constitution, one leadership, and one constituency, such a union would be hailed as a harbinger of harmony and victory. This has always been our ardent wish. Nevertheless, in entertaining it, we have never been anxious to compel a fellowship in appearance where none existed in fact. If we could now detect any good and valid reason why "The Union Woman's Suffrage Society" and "The American Woman's Suffrage Association" should not become one, we would as heartily urge these organizations to stay apart as we now urge them to come together. But our judgment is that the welfare of the cause will be promoted by a union of its friends. And it is toward the consummation of such a union that one of these societies has addressed to the other the following freindly epistle:

To the American Woman Suffrage Association:

Friends and Coworkers: We, the undersigned, a committee appointed by the Union Woman's Suffrage Society in New York, May, 1870, to confer with you on the subject of merging the two organizations into one, respectfully announce:

First, that in our judgment no difference exists between the objects and methods of the two societies, nor any good reason for keeping them apart;

Second, that the society we represent has invested us with full power to arrange with you a union of both under a single constitution and executive;

Third, that we ask you to appoint a committee of equal number and authority with our own, to consummate, if possible, this happy result.

Yours, in the common cause of woman's enfranchisement,

Laura Curtis Bullard, Gerrit Smith,[50] Sarah Pugh, Frederick Douglass, Mattie Griffith Browne, James W. Stillman, Isabella B. Hoover, Samuel J. May,[51] Charlotte B. Wilbour,[52] Josephine S. Griffing, Theodore Tilton, ex-officio.

In quoting the above letter, we desire to add that, if a union of the two societies shall be deemed desirable, and if the two committees shall agree upon a plan of consolidation, there would seem to be a propriety in choosing to the presidency of the new and combined association not a man but a woman.

With this single suggestion the editor of the *Independent*,[53] and president of "The Union Woman's Suffrage Society," is content to leave the plan of union to take its principal shaping from the hands of "The American Woman's Suffrage Association."

That this well meant effort at conciliation and union among reformers who aim to accomplish the same great object, and employ the same measures, and between whom there is no essential difference of opinion, ought to succeed few will deny, but, whether what ought to be, will be, in this case, is quite open to doubt. There cannot, however, be any harm in making the endeavor—Ed. *New National Era.*

*The New National Era,* November 24, 1870

### THE CONSTITUTION THE TITLE DEED TO WOMAN'S FRANCHISE

A letter with the above title has been addressed by Theodore Tilton, editor of the *Golden Age*, to Hon. Charles Sumner,[54] designed to demonstrate that by the 14th and 15th amendments, the Constitution of the United States has already invested American women with the right of suffrage.[55] The argument is the same in substance as that delivered in this city a few months ago by Mrs. Victoria C. Woodhull[56] and which was much commented upon at the time. Mr. Tilton has enlarged upon the argument, adorned it with his peculiarly brilliant style and from his premises his logic is not only clear, but irresistible. As a legal argument it is absolutely without a flaw. With a public sentiment at all favorable to the enfranchisement of women, we believe the courts of the country would readily adopt Mr. Tilton's reading of the Constitution, and declare women legally entitled to vote.

While we are quite aware that many will scout this new assumption in favor of women's rights as moonshine nonsense, or knavery, we see in it practical wisdom. It is wise for any reform to avail itself of any and every moral and legal force logically within its reach, by which it can attain a righteous end. No reform has any business to be multiplying obstacles against itself, and to assume that a change in the Constitution of the United States is necessary to woman's enfranchisement, is to put a vast obstacle in the way of woman's cause. The Constitution, except in presence of a concurrence of favorable conditions, which can only be hoped for in a century, is unchangeable as the laws of the Medes and Persians, and it is a great gain to woman's cause if it can be shown, as we think it has been, that no such alteration is necessary. Mrs. Woodhull and Mr. Tilton may be ridiculed and laughed at, but we should like to see any serious attempt to refute their arguments in favor of woman's Constitutional right to vote.

*The New National Era*, September 21, 1871


## WOMAN SUFFRAGE IN AUSTRIA

Few of those, we suppose, who oppose woman suffrage on the ground that it would result in the moral deterioration of woman, unfit her for the domestic relations and duties, unsex her, as it were, and produce a general dissolution of the existing order of society, are aware of the fact that in Austria women actually exercise the right of suffrage, and have exercised it since suffrage was granted to the people of the Empire. It is true that this right of suffrage is limited, and vastly different from our own universal suffrage; it is dependent on the possession of real estate; yet, since the law does not discriminate between man and woman, it is equally fair to either. Any woman, owning real estate in her own name, is a legal voter, while her husband may be disqualified in the absence of such a title. The system works quite satisfactorily, and none of the evils have been noticed which its opponents in this country and others predict as its inevitable consequences. Society has not been unhinged, and domestic peace is not perceptibly disturbed. Households are as well managed and children as well cared for as formerly. On the other side, it cannot be concealed that the zealous advocates of female suffrage who insist on it not only as the great and only remedy for all the real and imaginary grievances of woman, but as the measure that will radically cure almost all the evils and abuses of our social system, as the solution of the problems which puzzle the minds of social philosophers, would try in vain to point to such results in vindication of their theory. The condition of woman generally does not seem materially changed, and they are neither better nor worse off than in other civilized and tolerably well regulated countries. A noteworthy fact it is, however, that, in contradiction to the opinion so frequently asserted, that women constitute the conservative element of society, in Austria they are almost all enlisted on the side of freedom and progress. Even those belonging to the old high aristocracy, who own a large part of the landed estate of the Empire, cast their votes almost invariably in favor of the radical candidates. As fair representatives of culture and refinement, they contribute to illustrate the truth that education and knowledge are the great agents to liberate men from prejudice, superstition, and traditional notions, and to win them over to the side of liberty and progress.

*The New National Era*, December 7, 1871

## THE WOMAN'S RIGHTS CONVENTION

On Thursday and Friday, of last week, the ladies most prominent in the work of agitating the question of the right of women to participate as voters in the Government under which they live, held a convention in this city [Washington, D.C.] which was largely attended. The speeches were mainly made to prove that, under the fourteenth and fifteenth amendments to the Federal Constitution, women became entitled to the right of exercising the elective franchise. Speeches on this point were made by Susan B. Anthony, Elizabeth Cady Stanton, and others. The woman's suffrage cause is fast becoming fashionable, and prominent statesmen and lawyers are giving it respectful consideration all over the country. We would say to the women advocates of woman's suffrage that their flings at the negro and their constant parading him before their conventions as an ignorant monster possessing the ballot, while they are denied it, are of no real benefit to their cause. Mrs. Stanton, Miss Anthony, and their colaborers, claim that the ballot will elevate woman, that they are now slaves; the advocates of negro suffrage claimed that the ballot would elevate the negro; it has; they were ignorant, they are now making rapid strides in the way of education. The majority of the women of the country are ignorant on political questions nearly, if not quite, as ignorant as were the negroes before the ballot was given to them; but, like the negroes, they know right from wrong, and we fully believe that they need the ballot as well as does the negro. The flings at negro suffrage by the advocates of woman's suffrage are inconsistent with their claim that the governed are not justly governed without their consent, and smacks rather of an aristocratic feeling which finds expression in the claim that white women should have the ballot because they are better educated than black men.

*The New National Era*, January 23, 1873

## A WOMAN ASSISTANT EDITOR

"Three Distinguished Representative Men"
—Celia Logan[57] talks of Charles Sumner,
Frederick Douglass, and Donn Platt—
How she got a place on the *Capital*

All Americans return "home" sooner or later, and so did I, from Paris.

I was my own bread-winner, and in Washington.

Donn Platt and George Alfred Townsend had just started the *Capital*, but the latter had been called away suddenly, and I heard that Donn Platt was overwhelmed with work, mechanical as well as mental.

Women in Washington are necessarily self-reliant, with an ineradicable thirst for "promotion;" so, with much inward trembling and a great deal of outward confidence, I hurried to the office of the witty and caustic "D.P."

I was going to ask this much-dreaded man who scoffed at all, a bold, revolutionary question—"Could a woman be of any use on the *Capital*, were it only to look over the exchanges?"

Nerving my heart to the task, I entered his office and found that he was not there.

"Come in here and wait for him, if you want to see Donn Platt," cried a friendly voice in an opposite room. I turned. There sat between the door and the window, with the balmy May breezes ruffling his papers, Fred. Douglass.

His office and the place where he published his paper were in the front of the bulding where Donn Platt had made his venture of a "weekly."

Mr. Douglass and I were well acquainted, and I told him my reasons for wishing to see the distinguished humorist.

"What sort of a man is he?" I asked. "He is bad enough in his writings, but has he the moral courage to put a woman on his newspaper?"

Douglass replied, "I know no more fearless journalist anywhere. He cannot be bribed nor swayed by personal predilection. But he will soon be here and give you an answer."

"But I don't want an answer. I want the place. Do you think there is any chance of my getting it?"

"That I can't tell. He wants an assistant editor—"

"Editor! Oh, dear!"

"I think he will select one according to the individual's merits, without regard to sex. For that matter, you are not the first female applicant for the place, as you call it. Half the literary women of Washington—and their name is legion—have been here already, and whole shoals from the Treasury and other departments."

"Oh, gracious!" I groaned. "Small chance for me then!"

"I don't know that," he answered kindly. "Don't despond—don't lose heart! Look at me—not that I offer myself as an example, but I have overcome by preseverance, obstacles that even women do not have to contend with. I feel most for the women in this hard life-long battle for bread. They have against them the prejudices of sex. I had *color*. You have been educated. Thirty years ago I could neither read or write, for I was forbidden to learn. Thirty years ago I did not know a single letter, and I was then a man." He rose from his chair, his eyes blazing with indignation, and he tossed back his white locks.

The play of his fine features made a little thrill run through me. The dignity of his attitude, the majesty of his stature made Frederick Douglass look every inch a man. He continued: "Thirty years ago I was a slave, a miserable slave, with my wrongs eating into my heart. Thirty years ago," he reiterated, beating his broad breast in his growing excitement, "I did not own my own body! What may not you, what may not any other do after this?"

"The answer to that is easy," I replied. "There is but one Fred. Douglass."

"That's so," said a man, stepping in and shaking Douglass warmly by the hand. It was Charles Sumner!

He did not say: "This lady speaks but the truth, which statement I am prepared to corroborate, at any moment you may feel disposed to call upon me for testimony." He only said: "That's so."

Then he turned to me. He remembered me after all the years which had passed since we met in Paris. The great struggle which he had predicted had come and gone, leaving hardly any vestige of its ravages.

A little older he looked, a little more haggard; but the suave tones, the bland manner, the affability all remained unchanged.

While we chatted of old times there appeared another man in the very narrow passageway. It was Donn Platt.

As they stood there together, I thought I had never seen three more distinguished-looking representative men than the champion of liberty, the whilom bondsman, and the wit—for Donn Platt is more than a humorist, he is a wit. He is not funny for the public only—his wit bubbles over in his conversation, and he writes as easily as he talks, making no erasures, no revisions. I am certain of this, because afterwards I often saw him write, and oftener heard him talk. Because why? *I got that place.*

Celia Logan, in the *New York Daily Graphic*,
reprinted in *The New National Era*, May 14, 1874

## WHY I BECAME A "WOMAN'S RIGHTS MAN"

When the true history of the Anti-Slavery cause shall be written, women will occupy a large space in its pages; for the cause of the slave has been peculiarly woman's cause. Her heart and her conscience have supplied in large degree its motive and mainspring. Her skill, industry, patience, and perseverance have been wonderfully manifest in every trial hour. Not only did her feet run on "willing errands," and her fingers do the work which in large degree supplied the sinews of war, but her deep moral convictions, and her tender human sensibilities, found convincing and persuasive expression by her pen and her voice.

Observing woman's agency, devotion, and efficiency in pleading the cause of the slave, gratitude for this high service early moved me to give favorable attention to the subject of what is called "Woman's-rights" and caused me to be denominated a woman's-rights" man. I am glad to say that I have never been ashamed to be thus designated. Recognizing not sex nor physical strength, but moral intelligence and the ability to discern right from wrong, good from evil, and the power to choose between them, as the true basis of republican government, to which all are alike subject and all bound alike to obey, I was not long in reaching the conclusion that there was no foundation in reason or justice for woman's exclusion from the right of choice in the selection of the persons who should frame the laws, and thus shape the destiny of all the people, irrespective of sex.

In a conversation with Mrs. Elizabeth Cady Stanton when she was yet a young lady and an earnest Abolitionist, she was at the pains of setting before me in a very strong light the wrong and injustice of this exclusion. I could not meet her arguments except with the shallow plea of "custom," "natural division of duties," "indelicacy of woman's taking part in politics," the common talk of "woman's sphere," and the like, all of which that able woman, who was then no less logical than now, brushed away by those arguments which she has so often and effectively used since, and which no man has yet successfully refuted.

If intelligence is the only true and rational basis of government, it follows that that is the best government which draws its life and power from the largest sources of wisdom, energy, and goodness at its command. The force of this reasoning would be easily comprehended and readily assented to in any case involving the employment of physical strength. We should all see the folly and madness of attempting to accomplish with a part what could only be done with the united strength of the whole. Though this folly may be less apparent, it is just as real when one-half of the moral and intellectual power of the world is excluded from any voice or vote in civil government.

In this denial of the right to participate in government, not merely the degradation of woman and the perpetuation of a great injustice happens, but the maiming and repudiation of one-half of the moral and intellectual power of the government of the world. Thus far all human governments have been failures, for none have secured, except in a partial degree, the ends for which governments are instituted.

War, slavery, injustice and oppression, and the idea that might makes right have been uppermost in all such governments, and the weak, for whose protection governments are ostensibly created, have had practically no rights which the strong have felt bound to respect. The slayers of thousands have been exalted into heroes, and the worship of mere physical force has been considered glorious. Nations have been and still are but armed camps, expending their wealth and strength and ingenuity in forging weapons of destruction against each other; and while it may not be contended that the introduction of the feminine element in government would entirely cure this tendency to exalt might over right, many reasons can be given to show that woman's influence would greatly tend to check and modify this barbarous and destructive tendency.

At any rate, seeing that the male governments of the world have failed, it can do no harm to try the experiment of a government by man and woman united. But it is not my purpose to argue the question here, but simply to state in a brief way the ground of my espousal of the cause of woman's suffrage. I believed that the exclusion of my race from participation in government was not only wrong, but a great mistake, because it took from that race motives for high thought and endeavor and degraded them in the eyes of the world around them. Man derives a sense of his consequence in the world not merely subjectively, but objectively. If from the cradle through life the outside world brands a class as unfit for this or that work, the character of the class will come to resemble and conform to the character described. To find valuable qualities in our fellows, such qualities must be presumed and expected.

I would give woman a vote, give her a motive to qualify herself to vote, precisely as I insisted upon giving the colored man the right to vote; in order that she shall have the same motives for making herself a useful citizen as those in force in the case of other citizens. In a word, I have never yet been able to find one consideration, one argument, or suggestion in favor of man's right to participate in civil government which did not equally apply to the right of woman.

> *Life and Times of Frederick Douglass*
> (Hartford, Conn., 1881), pp. 473-482

## TO L. M. SAUNDERS (1885)

I have had the honor to receive your letter of the 15th instant, informing me that the Orr Bank has somewhat changed its decision in regard to leasing some of its rooms; that it was thought by some of the tenants, unwise to permit ladies of another color to come into the building and use it in common with ladies now in some of the rooms. You further state that you think that I can have the rooms if I will exclude colored ladies as clerks & letter writers.

You are also pleased to inform me that the objection raised is not to myself, personally, to all of which I respectfully beg leave to reply that I am somewhat surprised by the objection above stated. My application for rooms was natural. The building is an elegant one, admirably adapted to the wants of those who require offices for public business. They are so arranged that the occupants of one room need not interfere or incommode the occupant of any other, or prevent the best civil relations among them all. Each tenant is independent of any other. When Mr. A. applies for a room it is not necessary to consult Mr. B. who occupies another as to whether Mr. A. shall be admitted. They may be personal friends or personal enemies, but neither by the one nor by the other, is the civil rights of either impaired. They may occupy the same building as they occupy the same street, or the same street car, without detriment. In the light of these considerations, I might affect some surprise at the objection, but for the mention of color. That circumstance acts as a reversal of all civil, moral and Christian relations. It puts an end to the golden rule of doing to others as we would that others should do unto us and turns loose all the elements of pride, prejudice and selfishness. The objection is to colored lady clerks. It was not my purpose to employ any such. I shall probably have no occasion to employ any such. But you can easily see that I could not honorably promise their exclusion. I am among those who rejoice at every honorable vocation offered and embraced by white ladies, and I am equally happy when such vocations are open to colored ladies. I have also the highest respect for poor white ladies who earn their bread by hard work at the desk of the type writer. I unite with them when they pray, "Give us this day our daily bread." But I cannot unite with them when they would exclude any lady of whatever color from the same means of earning her daily bread. "That mercy I to others show, that mercy show to me."

The spirit that would drive a colored type writer out of your building, simply for being colored, would drive her into the penitentiary or out of the world.

Why should the ladies in your building be more averse to the presence of colored ladies than are the ladies employed in the Treasury Department, the Interior, the P.O. or other departments of the government? Are they more cultivated, refined and wealthy? Colored ladies are employed in all those departments and some of the white ladies are employed in divisions under the superivison of colored heads.

I venture to say that in no other country of the civilized world could an objection, similar to yours, be raised to leasing me a room in any public building. When a Democratic Pres[ident] makes no such distinction, it seems a little out of place for anything with the name of Ohio attached to it, to set up an objection so undemocratic as that raised in your letter.

The white ladies in your building ought to know that because they work for their bread there are other white ladies so proud of their wealth & standing as to scorn to associate with such clerks & type writers as themselves. In objecting to colored type writers, they are cherishing a spirit of pride & selfishness which reaches upon themselves. But I have said enough and part with you in the full assurance that truth & justice are patient, long suffering and per-sistent, and that they will, in the end, prevail.

I shall reserve our correspondence, and if you do not object, it may be published.

Respectfully yours,
Frederick Douglass

Ms., Frederick Douglass Papers, Douglass Memorial Home,
Anacostia, District of Columbia.


## THE WOMAN'S SUFFRAGE MOVEMENT
## ADDRESS BEFORE WOMAN SUFFRAGE ASSOCIATION, APRIL 1888

Mrs. President, Ladies and Gentlemen:

I come to this platform with unusual diffidence. Although I have long been identified with the Woman's Suffrage movement, and have often spoken in its favor, I am somewhat at a loss to know what to say on this really great and uncommon occasion, where so much has been said.

When I look around on this assembly, and see the many able and eloquent women, full of the subject, ready to speak, and who only need the opportunity to impress this audience with their views and thrill them with "thoughts that breathe and words that burn," I do not feel like taking up more than a very small space of your time and attention, and shall not. I would not, even now, presume to speak, but for the circumstance of my early connection with the cause, and of having been called upon to do so by one whose voice in this Council we all gladly obey. Men have very little business here as speakers, anyhow; and if they come here at all they should take back benches and wrap themselves in silence. For this is an International Council, not of men, but of women, and woman should have all the say in it. This is her day in court.

I do not mean to exalt the intellect of woman above man's; but I have heard many men speak on this subject, some of them the most eloquent to be found anywhere in the country; and I believe no man, however gifted with thought and speech, can voice the wrongs and present the demands of women with the skill and effect, with the power and authority of woman herself. The man struck is the man to cry out. Woman knows and feels her wrongs as man cannot know and feel them, and she also knows as well as he can know, what measures are needed to redress them. I grant all the claims at this point. She is her own best representative. We can neither speak for her, nor vote for her, nor act for her, nor be responsible for her; and the thing for men to do in the premises is just to get out of her way and give her the fullest opportunity to exercise all the powers inherent in her individual personality, and allow her to do it as herself shall elect to exercise them. Her right to be and to do is as full, complete and perfect as the right of any man on earth. I say of her, as I say of the colored people. "Give her fair play, and hands off."

There was a time when, perhaps, we men could help a little. It was when this woman suffrage cause was in its cradle, when it was not big enough to go alone, when it had to be taken in the arms of its mother from Seneca Falls, N.Y., to Rochester, N.Y., for baptism. I then went along with it and offered my services to help it, for then it needed help; but now it can afford to dispense with me and all of my sex. Then its friends were few—now its friends are many. Then it was wrapped in obscurity—now it is lifted in sight of the whole civilized world, and people of all lands and languages give it their hearty support. Truly the change is vast and wonderful.

I thought my eye of faith was tolerably clear when I attended those meetings in Seneca Falls and Rochester, but it was far too dim to see at the end of forty years a result so imposing as this International Council, and to see yourself and Miss Anthony alive and active in its proceedings. Of course, I expected to be alive myself, and am not surprised to find myself so; for such is, perhaps, the presumption and arrogance common to my sex. Nevertheless, I am very glad to see you here to-day, and to see this grand assembly of women. I am glad that you are its president. No manufactured "boom," or political contrivance, such as make presidents elsewhere, has made you president of this assembly of women in this Capital of the Nation. You hold your place by reason of eminent fitness, and I give you joy that your life and labors in the cause of woman are thus crowned with honor and glory. This I say in spite of the warning given us by Miss Anthony's friend against mutual admiration.

There may be some well-meaning people in this audience who have never attended a woman suffrage convention, never heard a woman suffrage speech, never read a woman suffrage newspaper, and they may be surprised that those who speak here do not argue the question. It may be kind to tell them that our cause has passed beyond the period of arguing. The demand of the hour is not argument, but assertion, firm and inflexible assertion, assertion which has more than the force of an argument. If there is any argument to be made, it must be made by the opponents, not by the friends of woman suffrage. Let those who want argument examine the ground upon which they base their claim to the right to vote. They will find that there is not one reason, not one consideration, which they can urge in support of man's claim to vote, which does not equally support the right of woman to vote.

There is to-day, however, a special reason for omitting argument. This is the end of the fourth decade of the woman suffrage movement, a kind of jubilee which naturally turns our minds to the past.

Ever since this Council has been in session, my thoughts have been reverting to the past. I have been thinking, more or less, of the scene presented forty years ago in the little Methodist Church at Seneca Falls, the manger in which this organized suffrage movement was born. It was a very small thing then. It was not then big enough to be abused or loud enough to make itself heard outside, and only a few of those who saw it had any notion that the little thing would live. I have been thinking, too, of the strong conviction, the noble courage, the sublime faith in God and man it required at that time to set this suffrage ball in motion. The history of the world has given to us many sublime undertakings, but none more sublime than this. It was a great thing for the friends of peace to organize in opposition to war; it was a great thing for the friends of temperance to organize against intemperance; it was a great thing for humane people to organize in opposition to slavery; but it was a much greater thing, in view of all the circumstances, for woman to organize herself in opposition to her exclusion from participation in government. The reason is obvious. War, intemperance and slavery are open, undisguised, palpable evils. The best feelings of human nature revolt at them. We could easily make men see the misery, the debasement, the terrible suffering caused by intemperance; we could easily make men see the desolation wrought by war and the hell-black horrors of chattel slavery; but the case was different in the movement for woman suffrage. Men took for granted all that could be said against intemperance, war and slavery. But no such advantage was found in the beginning of the cause of suffrage for women. On the contrary, everything in her condition was supposed to be lovely, just as it should be. She had no rights denied, no wrongs to redress. She herself had no suspicion but that all was going well with her. She floated along on the tide of life as her mother and grandmother had done before her, as in a dream of Paradise. Her wrongs, if she had any, were too occult to be seen, and too light to be felt. It required a daring voice and a determined hand to awake her from this delightful dream and call the nation to account for the rights and opportunities of which it was depriving her. It was well understood at the beginning that woman would not thank us for disturbing her by this call to duty, and it was known that man would denounce and scorn us for such a daring innovation upon the established order of things. But this did not appeal or delay the word and work.

At this distance of time from that convention at Rochester, and in view of the present position of the question, it is hard to realize the moral courage it required to launch this unwelcome movement. Any man can be brave when the danger is over, go to the front when there is no resistance, rejoice when the battle is fought and the victory is won; but it is not so easy to venture upon a field untried with one-half the whole world against you, as these women did.

Then who were we, for I count myself in, who did this thing? We were few in numbers, moderate in resources, and very little known in the world. The most that we had to commend us was a firm faith that the right must ultimately prevail. But the case was well considered. Let no man imagine that the step was taken recklessly and thoughtlessly. Mrs. Stanton had dwelt upon it at least six years before she declared it in the Rochester convention. Walking with her from the house of Joseph and Thankful Southwick, two of the noblest people I ever knew, Mrs. Stanton, with an earnestness that I shall never forget, unfolded her views on this woman question precisely as she has in this Council. This was six and forty years ago, and it was not until six years after, that she ventured to make her formal, pronounced and startling demand for the ballot. She had, as I have said, considered well, and knew something of what would be the cost of the reform she was inaugurating. She knew the ridicule, the rivalry, the criticism and the bitter aspersions which she and her co-laborers would have to meet and to endure. But she saw more clearly than most of us that the vital point to be made prominent, and the one that included all others, was the ballot, and she bravely said the word. It was not only necessary to break the silence of woman and make her voice heard, but she must have a clear, palpable and comprehensive measure set before her, one worthy of her highest ambition and her best exertions, and hence the ballot was brought to the front.

There are few facts in my humble history to which I look back with more satisfaction than to the fact, recorded in the history of the Woman Suffrage Movement, that I was sufficiently enlightened at that early day, and when only a few years from slavery, to support your resolution for woman suffrage. I have done very little in this world in which to glory except this one act—and I certainly glory in that. When I ran away from slavery, it was for myself; when I advocated emancipation, it was for my people; but when I stood up for the rights of woman, self was out of the question, and I found a little nobility in the act.

In estimating the forces with which this suffrage cause has had to contend during these forty years, the fact should be remembered that relations of long standing beget a character in the parties to them in favor of their continuance. Time itself is a conservative power—a very conservative power. One shake of his hoary locks will sometimes paralyze the hand and palsy the tongue of the reformer. The relation of man to woman has the advantage of all the ages behind it. Those who oppose a readjustment of this relation tell us that what is always was and always will be, world without end. But we have heard this old argument before, and if we live very long we shall hear it again. When any aged error shall be assailed, and any old abuse is to be removed, we shall meet the same old argument. Man has been so long the king and woman the subject— man has been so long accustomed to command and woman to obey— that both parties to the relation have been hardened into their respective places, and thus has been piled up a mountain of iron against woman's enfranchisement.

The same thing confronted us in our conflicts with slavery. Long years ago Henry Clay[58] said, on the floor of the American Senate, "I know there is a visionary dogma that man cannot hold property in man," and, with a brow of defiance, he said, "That is property which the law makes property. Two hundred years of legislation has sanctioned and sanctified negro slaves as property." But neither the power of time nor the might of legislation has been able to keep life in that stupendous barbarism.

The universality of man's rule over woman is another factor in the resistance to the woman suffrage movement. We are pointed to the fact that men have not only always ruled over women, but that they do so rule everywhere, and they easily think that a thing that is done everywhere must be right. Though the fallacy of this reasoning is too transparent to need refutation, it still exerts a powerful influence. Even our good Brother Jasper yet believes, with the ancient church, that the sun "do move," notwithstanding all the astronomers of the world are against him. One year ago I stood on the Pincio in Rome and witnessed the unveiling of the Statue of Galileo.[59] It was an imposing sight. At no time before had Rome been free enough to permit such a statue to be placed within her walls. It is now there, not with the approval of the Vatican. No priest took part in the ceremonies. It was all the work of laymen. One or two priests passed the statue with averted eyes, but the great truths of the solar system were not angry at the sight, and the same will be true when woman shall be clothed, as she will yet be, with all the rights of American citizenship.

All good causes are mutually helpful. The benefits acruing from this movement for the equal rights of woman are not confined or limited to woman only. They will be shared by every effort to promote the progress and welfare of mankind everywhere and in all ages. It was an example and a prophecy of what can be accomplished against strongly opposing forces, against time-hallowed abuses, against deeply intrenched error, against world-wide usage, and against the settled judgment of mankind, by a few earnest women, clad only in the panoply of truth, and determined to live and die in what they considered a righteous cause.

I do not forget the thoughtful remark of our president in the opening address to this International Council,[60] reminding us of the incompleteness of our work. The remark was wise and timely. Nevertheless, no man can compare the present with the past, the obstacles that then opposed us, and the influences that now favor us, the meeting in the little Methodist chapel forty years ago, and the Council in this vast theatre to-day, without admitting that woman's cause is already a brilliant success. But, however this may be, and whatever the future may have in store for us, one thing is certain—this new revolution in human thought will never go backward. When a great truth once gets abroad in the world, no power on earth can imprison it, or prescribe its limits, or suppress it. It is bound to go on till it becomes the thought of the world. Such was born with it. It was hers before she comprehended it. It is inscribed upon all the powers and faculties of our soul, and no custom, law nor usage can ever destroy it. Now that it has got fairly fixed in the minds of the few, it is bound to become fixed in the minds of the many, and be supported at last by a great cloud of witnesses, which no man can number and no power can withstand.

The women who have thus far carried on this agitation have already embodied and illustrated Theodore Parker's[61] three grades of human greatness. The first is greatness in executive and administrative ability; second, greatness in the ability to organize; and, thirdly, in the ability to discover truth. Wherever these three elements of power are combined in any movement, there is a reasonable ground to believe in its final success; and these elements of power have been manifest in the women who have had the movement in hand from the beginning. They are seen in the fervid eloquence and downright earnest with which women advocate their cause. They are seen in the profound attention with which woman is heard in her own behalf. They are seen in the steady growth and onward march of the movement, and they will be seen in the final triumph of woman's cause, not only in this country, but throughout the world.

*The Woman's Journal,* April 14, 1888

EMANCIPATION OF WOMEN
SPEECH AT THE TWENTIETH ANNUAL MEETING OF THE
NEW ENGLAND WOMAN SUFFRAGE ASSOCIATION,
TREMONT TEMPLE, BOSTON, MAY 28, 1888

Mrs. Stone then introduced Frederick Douglass:
ADDRESS OF FREDERICK DOUGLASS.
*Madame President, Ladies and Gentlemen:*

While I esteem it an honor to stand on this New England woman suffrage platform, I do not feel that I have a right to the prominence you have been pleased to give me in this your proceedings, by calling me at this time. It is, perhaps, about time that I should decline to be a speaker on occasions like the present. Having survived the anti-slavery conflict, and lived to rejoice in the victory over slavery, and being no longer as young as I once was, I am a little too late for efficiency and prominence in the great cause you have in hand. My special mission in the world, if I ever had any, was the emancipation and enfranchisement of the negro. Mine was a great cause. Yours is a much greater cause, since it comprehends the liberation and elevation of one-half of the whole human family. Happily, however, I have two good reasons for coming upon this platform to-night. The first is, I live near the city of Washington; not a very strong reason, perhaps, but I come to you from an atmosphere largely pervaded with the woman suffrage sentiment, and am so much in sympathy with it, that it is more difficult to be silent than to speak in its favor. In the second place, this cause has a valid claim upon my "service and labor," outside of its merits. The New England Woman Suffrage Association is composed in part of the noble women who dared to speak for the freedom of the slave, at a time when it required far more courage to do so than is required to speak in the woman suffrage cause at this day.

I have said I reside near Washington, the capital of the nation. Let me say a word about that city in connection with this and kindred reforms. Its behavior of late has been worthy of praise. In the old times, prior to the war and the abolition of slavery, there was no room in it for woman suffrage or negro suffrage or many other good things. It shuddered at the thought of a new idea—slavery, the slave trade, slave auctions, horse-racing, duels, and revivals of religion were the popular excitements in the Washington of that day. But now old Washington has passed away, and a new Washington has come into existence. Under our much-abused Gov. Sheppard, its physical features have been visibly improved, and under the influence of Northern ideas, its moral features have equally improved. The time is not distant, I hope, when it will symbolize all that is good, great, glorious and free, and much of the glory of that result will be due to the efforts of women.

It will be next year the theatre of a grand international exposition. Its attractive power is destined to increase with every year, and Boston itself as a reformatory centre may begin to look to its laurels.

Boston was once known as the hot-bed of abolitionism. Washington, if it keeps well on its way, will soon become the hot-bed of woman suffrage. One of the most imposing demonstrations in favor of the rights and dignity of woman was held there only a few weeks ago. You may have heard something of this before. Women from the East, women from the West, women from the North, and women from the South; women from home and women from abroad, met there in International Council, and united in a solemn demand for a larger measure of liberty, and a fuller participation in the government of the world, than has ever yet been accorded to woman. No assemblage to my knowledge, can be pointed to in the history of this republic, which ever presented a more sublime spectacle than did this International Council. Its presence was an argument in favor of its cause. Its refinement, earnestness, ability and dignity repelled criticism and overcame opposition. In the hope and enthusiasm it inspired, some of us were made to think, or rather to feel, that the year of woman's jubilee had already dawned.

But this Council has adjourned, and although its beneficent influence will continue to be felt far and wide over the world, we are still confronted with the same old conflict, and must fight it out on the line of agitation though it shall take a century. There is still a delinquent, tardy, and reluctant Massachusetts to be converted, there is still a mass of bigotry and superstition to overcome. There is still a Methodist Episcopal Conference confronting us and barring the way to woman's progress, as it once barred the way to emancipation. There is still a great nation to be brought to a knowledge of the truth. We are not to be appalled by the magnitude of the work, or discouraged by this or any other form of opposition.

We old abolitionists never allowed ourselves to be dismayed by repulses, however grievous. Those engaged in this cause are of the self-same material. In some respects this woman suffrage movement is but a continuance of the old anti-slavery movement. We have the same sources of opposition to contend with, and we must meet them with the same spirit and determination, and with much the same arguments which we employed against what Charles Sumner called the "seven-headed barbarism of slavery."

In reform, as in war, it is always a point gained to know just where the enemy is, and just what he is about. It is not easy to deal with an enemy in the dark. It was a great thing for the abolition cause, fifty years ago, when the Methodist Episcopal Conference at Cincinnati declared itself opposed to abolitionism, and that it had no right, wish, or intention to abolish slavery. It is now equally something to know that this same organization takes its stand against the movement for the equal rights of woman in its ecclesiastical assemblies. That older conference was not able, by its opposition to abolitionism, to save slavery, nor will this later conference be able to continue the degradation of woman, by denying her a voice and a vote in its councils. The Methodist Church is rich in resources, but it cannot well afford to enforce this Mahometan idea of woman upon American women—an idea in which woman has no recognized moral, social, or religious existence. In the mosques of the East, her presence among the faithful is held a defilement. She is deemed incapable of self-direction—a body without a soul. No more distressing thing confronted us during our recent tour in Egypt than this social and religious annihilation of women. Religion there strikes woman dead. Her face is not to be seen; her voice is not to be heard; her moral influence is not to be exerted. She is cushioned, cabined, confined and guarded, and treated more like a criminal than like an innocent person. She sees the world only through a veil, or from behind a lattice-work. She is constantly under the surveillance of a sentinel, wearing the human form, but destitute of all manly sympathy. This Methodist attempt to exclude woman from the conference of the church, has in it a strong element of this Mahometan idea of the proper sphere and treatment of woman.

Whatever may be said of the pious Mahometan, men and women here will ask, and demand to know, what harm could possibly come to the Methodist Church and its ministers, from the presence of a few or many Christian women in its conference? The sexes meet together in prayer-meeting, in class-meeting, in "love feast," and in the great congregations of the church. Why should these gospel preachers, who mingle everywhere else in the church with women, be afraid to meet women in their conferences? What work have they to do there which women should not know? I will press this question no further, but I call upon the Methodist Church to assist us in separating woman's condition in America as far apart from her condition in Egypt as the east is from the west. We have heard a great deal of late as to what Christianity has done for woman. We have a right to call upon these Christian ministers to show that what has been done, has not been done in spite of the church, but in accordance with its teachings. One thing is certain, when the chains of woman shall be broken, when she shall become the recognized equal of man, and is put into the full enjoyment of all the rights of an American citizen, as she will be, church and ministry will be the first to claim the honor of the victory, and to say, "We did it!"

It is hardly necessary for me to say, after what I have already said, that I am a radical woman suffrage man. I was such a man nearly fifty years ago. I had hardly brushed the dust of slavery from my feet and stepped upon the free soil of Massachusetts, when I took the suffrage side of this question. Time, thought and experience have only increased the strength of my conviction. I believe equally in its justice, in its wisdom, and in its necessity.

But, as I understand the matter, woman does not ask man for the right of suffrage. That is something which man has no power to give. Rights do not have their source in the will or the grace of man. They are not such things as he can grant or withhold according to his sovereign will and pleasure. All that woman can properly ask man to do in this case, and all that man can do, is to get out of the way, to take his obstructive forces of fines and imprisonment and his obstructive usages out of the way, and let woman express her sentiments at the polls and in the government, equally with himself. Give her fair play and let her alone.

But we are told that suffrage is not a right, that it is neither a right for man nor for woman, but that it is simply a privilege. I do not know when or by whom this startling discovery was made, but it is evidently deemed very important and highly satisfactory by the opponents of woman suffrage.

Well, for argument's sake, let it be conceded that suffrage is not a natural right, but that it is simply a privilege, something that is created and exists only by conventional arrangement; something that can be granted or withheld at the option of those who make it a privilege. I say let all this be conceded, which I do not concede. Several important questions must be answered by those who support this pretension, before the friends of woman suffrage can be silenced or be made to accept it as final.

In the first place we have a right to know by what authority, human or divine, suffrage was made a privilege and not a right; we have a right to know when, where, how, and in the light of what doctrine of human liberty, suffrage was made a privilege and not a right. We have a right to know if men, acting alone, have the right to decide what is right, and what is privilege where their action in the case is to determine the position of woman. We have a right to know, if suffrage is simply a privilege, by what right the exercising of that privilege is conferred only upon men. If it is a privilege, we have the right to know why woman is excluded. If it is a privilege, we have the right to know why woman is not as fully, fairly entitled to exercise that privilege as man himself.

After all, we see that nothing has been gained by the opponents of woman suffrage, by sheltering themselves behind this assumption that suffrage is a privilege and not a right. The argument is an old one, and has been answered a thousand times, and will, perhaps, have to be answered a thousand times more, before woman suffrage shall be the law of the land.

I suppose we must do here, as was done in the case of the anti-slavery agitation, give line upon line and precept upon precept, as we had to do forty years ago.

Woman's claim to the right of equal participation in government with man, has its foundation in the nature and personality of woman and in the admitted doctrine of American liberty and in the authority and structure of our Republican government. When the rich man wanted someone sent from the dead to warn his brothers against coming where he was, he was told if they heard not Moses and the prophets, neither would they be persuaded though one rose from the dead. Now our Moses and our prophets, so far as the rights and privileges of American citizens are concerned, are the framers of the Declaration of Independence. If the American people will not hear these, they will not be persuaded though one rose from the dead.

According to the Declaration of Independence and to the men who signed that great charter of human liberty, all rightful powers of government are derived from the consent of the governed.

No man has yet been able to state when, where and how woman has ever given her consent to be deprived of all participation in the government under which she lives, or why women should be excepted from the principles of the American Declaration of Independence. We are told that man derived his authority thus to disenfranchise woman from Nature; well, we should all have great respect for Nature. We cannot too often listen to her voice and learn the lessons she teaches. She is the great storehouse of knowledge, wisdom and truth. It was here that Hooker learned that beautiful sentiment that law has her seat in the bosom of God and her voice is the harmony of the universe. I think the friends of woman suffrage have no reason to refuse to have the question of their rights tried in this august court we call Nature.

Let us begin then with Nature in the family. This is the starting-point of life, the natural starting-point of organized society and of the State. Here are a son and a daughter in the same household. They have nursed at the same breast in their infancy; they have been supplied from the same board; they have talked, sung, prayed, and played together on equal terms in their youth; they have grown into manhood and womanhood together; in a word, they have been equal members of the same family together all their young lives with substantially the same rights and privileges in the common family; they have received the same moral and intellectual training, and have enjoyed the same freedom of thought and expressions around the family board—the right to ask and to answer questions. They are equal in moral and intellectual endowments, or if not so equal, the one is as likely to be superior as the other, the daughter as the son, the sister as the brother. Now the question to be answered at this point is just this: At what time and under what conditions does nature step in to change the relations of these two people and make the son and brother the ruler of this daughter and sister? When does Nature say that he shall elect law-makers, and make laws, institute governments, define for her the metes and bounds of her liberty, and that she, a rational creature like himself, shall have no voice or vote in determining any question concerning the government under which she, equally with him, is to live? They were equal in the cradle, equal in the family, equal in childhood, equal in youth, equal at maturity, equal in the right to life, to liberty, and to the pursuit of happiness. I demand to know, then, what fiat of nature, what moral earthquake from below, or what thunder-bolt from above, has driven these two people asunder—raised one to the sky and struck the other to earth—one to freedom and the other to slavery. The only answer that Nature is alleged to give here in opposition to woman, is one which no just and generous man can or should accept, for it bases a moral and intellectual conclusion—one which excludes woman from all freedom of choice in the affairs of government—upon a purely physical fact. The logic is that man is physically stronger than woman, and that he has the right to make her a subject of his will; that since she cannot shoulder a musket and fight, she shall not select a ballot and vote—that though she may have the ability to think, she shall not have the right to express her thought and give effect to her thought by her vote. There is no getting away from the conclusion here other than that the essence of this anti-woman suffrage doctrine is that might makes right. It is the right of the usurper, the slave-holder, the tyrant, the robber and pirate—a right which better befits wild beasts than reasoning men and women—a right which no woman ought to admit and no man should claim. The only thing that saves it from execration is the fact that men are too humane and too civilized to make their practice conform to the full measure of their theory.. They deny rights, but admit influence. She may not vote herself, they say, but she may influence the man who does vote, and it is precisely this which constitutes the vice of this relation, for it gives influence and excludes responsibility. A sense of responsibility is an essential element in all our exertions and relations. We need it; woman needs it, not less than man, to work out the best results of her conduct. Divest woman of power and you divest her of a sense of responsibility and duty—two of the essential attributes of all useful exertion and existence.

In tracing the moral and intellectual progress of mankind from barbarism to civilization, we see that any and every advance, however simple and reasonable, has been sternly resisted. It appears that the more simple the proposition of reform, the more stern and passionate has been the resistance. Victory has always been found, when found at all, on the other side of the battlefield.

The proposition underlying the anti-slavery movement was one of the plainest that ever dropped from the lips of man. It was so simple and self-evident that argument seemed a waste of breath, and appeal an insult to the understanding, and yet this simple proposition held within itself an explosive force more powerful than dynamite—a force which divided and drove asunder the nation, rent it in twain at the centre, and filled the land with hostile armies. The fundamental proposition of anti-slavery was simply this: Every man is himself, or in other words, is *his* self, or, which is the same thing, every man is the rightful owner of himself. Nothing could be plainer than this, yet press and pulpit, church and State, saint and sinner, North and South, denounced the proposition as full of mischief and one to be put down at all hazards. Man's right to his religious faith, to believe what he could not do otherwise than believe, shared the same fate and filled Europe with nearly a century of war. With these and other and similar examples before us we are not to think it strange that the proposition to enfranchise woman, to clothe her with all the rights and dignity of American citizenship, meets with resistance.

The fundamental proposition of the woman suffrage movement is scarcely less simple than that of the anti-slavery movement. It assumes that woman is herself. That she belongs to herself, just as fully as man belongs to himself—that she is a person and has all the attributes of personality that can be claimed by man, and that her rights of person are equal in all respects to those of man. She has the same number of senses that distinguish man, and is like man a subject of human government, capable of understanding, obeying and being affected by law. That she is capable of forming an intelligent judgment as to the character of public men and public measures and she may exercise her right of choice in respect both to the law and the lawmakers. Than all this nothing could be more simple or more reasonable.

The generation that has come on the stage since the war can hardly now realize, in view of the fundamental principles of American government, that slavery ever existed here, that the pulpit and press, that the church and the State ever defended it. So, when this battle for woman suffrage shall have been fought and the victory won, men will marvel at the injustice and stupidity which so long deprived American women of the ballot.

Let me say in conclusion, if human nature is totally depraved, if men and women are incapable of thinking or doing anything but evil and that continually, if the character of this government will inevitably be the expression of this universal and innate depravity—then the less men and women have to do with government the better. We should abandon our Republican government, cease to elect men to office, and place ourselves squarely under the Czar of Russia, the Pope of Rome, or some other potentate who governs by divine right. But if, on the contrary, human nature is more virtuous than vicious, as I believe it is, if governments are best supported by the largest measure of virtue within their reach, if women are equally virtuous with men, if the whole is greater than a part, if the sense and sum of human goodness in man and woman combined is greater than in that of either alone and separate, then the government that excludes women from all participation in its creation, administration, and perpetuation, maims itself, deprives itself of one-half of all that is wisest and best for its usefulness, success and perfection.[62]

*The Woman's Journal*, June 2, 1888

## ADDRESS BEFORE WOMAN SUFFRAGE CONVENTION (UNDATED)

Ladies and Gentlemen: When I received from your honored President an invitation to be present this evening, I neither expected nor aspired to come before you at this important state of your proceedings. I am but only an humble layman in the woman suffrage church. I do not know that I am in good and regular standing, even that much of it which holds its annual meetings in the place where I reside. Yet I am sure that I am thoroughly in sympathy with the woman suffrage movement, and am working for its advancement. I can say however without the slightest affection of diffidence, that I preferred that some other person—some one of the noble women I see around me—who by ability, eloquence and devotion to this cause is entitled to and should occupy the post of honor now allotted to me. Man has at best a very moderate claim to prominence on this platform. He may well feel himself sufficiently honored if admitted even to take a back seat. He is the sinner. Woman is the preacher. She is her own best advocate. On such occasions as this, she holds the post of honor and the post of usefulness by virtue of her moral sovereignty, and by right of her superior efficiency. No man, however eloquent, can speak for woman as woman can for herself.

Nevertheless, I hold that this cause is not altogether and exclusively woman's cause. It is the cause of human brotherhood as well as the cause of human sisterhood, and both must rise and fall together. Woman cannot be elevated without elevating man, and man cannot be depressed without depressing woman also.

I used to say if you want to keep a man out of the mud, you should black his boots. If you want him to expect something of himself you must expect something of him. I say the same of woman. Throw around her the robes of power and the dignity of complete citizenship, make her responsible for the good or ill of the Republic, make her see that she is something more than a cipher in this world, and she will develop a character higher than is now dreamed of in her present dwarfed condition. She will feel her responsibility. She will inform herself on the questions uppermost in the state, and qualify herself to pass upon them and be more fully a companion of man, than ever before. Exalted as she now is in this country over the women of the Eastern world, she will be more exalted when she shall, as she certainly will, achieve her complete citizenship and suffrage.

Ms., Frederick Douglass Papers, Library of Congress
Manuscripts Division, Washington, D.C.

## WOMAN SUFFRAGE MOVEMENT
## ADDRESS BEFORE BETHEL LITERARY SOCIETY
## (UNDATED)

I propose to read to you, this evening, an essay on the Woman Suffrage movement, a subject upon which much has been said and written of late, but which has not, I believe, received any formal discussing in the forum of the Bethel Literary Society.[63]

Forty years ago woman was hardly recognized as a factor in civilization. She had no public voice whatever. So far as the public was concerned, she was silent as the grave. For her, the stillness and solitude were so deep and unbroken that she started at the sound of her own voice, and shuddered at the shock she was giving her public hearers. It is true that in church she was allowed to sing the thoughts of others, and in the theatre she was allowed to declaim the writings of others, but she was not accepted either as a public teacher or preacher. Public sentiment proclaimed silence as her mission, and specified her work, to cook, wash, iron, sew, knit, weave, darn, and take care of children. This, in those days, was called *woman's sphere*. Fathers, husbands, brothers, and sons, shuddered at the thought of daughters, wives, sisters, and sweethearts standing before a multitude of men and women and making themselves heard in speech. All manner of ridicule and ribaldry was poured upon woman conventions and other demonstrations. But a vast and wonderful change has been wrought in the public mind, upon this as well as upon many other subjects in our day. There is now no language nor speech where woman's voice is not heard. The elite of the land now listen with respect and admiration to the wisdom and eloquence of woman. In respect of her right of speech, her victory is complete. She is today recognized, not only as an angel of beauty, but of temperance and order, the criterion of morals and manners. It will be seen, in this study of this movement, that it has conformed to the law of evolution. It was first the blade, then the ear, and then, the full corn in the ear. The boldest pioneers in the movement did not think, at first, of asking for the right of suffrage. To this great height, they had not been lifted. What they wanted, first of all, and most of all, was that greatest of all rights, the right of speech, the right to utter their pent up feelings and the convictions of their newly awakened souls; to make a fiery protest against the fetters with which custom, bigotry and superstition had for ages bound them. Naturally enough, theirs was to the common ear, the wild alarm cry of revolt, a shout of defiance from the barricades of rebellion to the forts and arsenals of social order and conservatism. It was the uprising of one half of the human race against the opinions and customs of the other half, and if successful, it will be the most stupendous revolution the world has ever witnessed.

At the beginning of this crusade for a larger measure of liberty, only a few women dared to show their hands. In this, as in all other great movements, the day of shame precedes the day of glory.

The foremost, bravest, and most conspicuous of those who espoused the cause, were Angelina and Sarah Grimké,[64] Abby Kelley,[65] and Lucretia Mott. Against popular usage, against prejudice, and the vulgar and tumultous crowd, these brave women rose in grandeur and glory like the rainbow, radiant above the black and howling storm.

It is said that this movement can never succeed, that woman can never be enfranchised. I do not now affirm that she can and will be, but I do say that he is a bold man who will affirm that woman will not some day vote.

In judging of the possible success of this cause, we should not measure its progress by the distance at which it stands from its ultimate object, or by the obstacles it has yet to overcome, but rather from the point from which it started and the obstacles it has already overcome. If much remains to be done, much has already been done. Archimedes only wanted a place for the fulcrum of his lever, to move the world.

This lever woman has already gained. She can speak, write and agitate, and these are more than swords, guns and dynamite.

"Weapons of war she has cast from the battle,

Truth is her armor, her watchword is LOVE."

If she conquers, it will be by these mild arms—in controlling the thoughts and feelings of men.

Her first demand was for speech. Her next was for education, and the next was for an enlargement of her industrial vocations.

She has measureably gained all three. Thirty years ago there were about thirty employments open to women. Now, there are more than three hundred open to her.

The cry for bread is a terrible cry. It came from dark cellars, from dilapidated garrets, from fireless hearthstones, from widows and orphans, where glassy-eyed hunger sat, helpless and desolate, and where no manly arm was extended to save. It was a scream to man to give virtuous womanhood leave to toil, and to rescue her from want and crime.

Victor Hugo[66] has said many true and touching things of the suffering poor, but he has never said any thing more true and pathetic than this: *"He who has seen the misery of man only, has seen nothing. He must see the misery of woman. He who has seen the misery of woman only, has seen nothing. He must see the misery of childhood." Wretchedness here, transcends all wretchedness elsewhere.*

A thousand doors are open to man, where one is open to woman.

Ms., Frederick Douglass Papers, Library of Congress,
Manuscripts Division, Washington, D.C.

## ADDRESS TO MEMBERS OF THE WOMEN'S LEAGUE (UNDATED)

Mr. President and Members of the Women's League:

It is with an interest of far deeper than ordinary significance, that I acknowledge the kindness which welcomes my expressions of sympathy and interest in the efforts and purposes of your League.

This interest is intensified, and, solemnized and sanctified by the remembrance that I stand in the place of one whose presence would have been like the stretching of a home-tent over your heads; one whose very presence, without a single word, was a pillar of support to any cause.

We recognize the importance and significance of this occasion, the National expression of your Union with a movement which is, in itself, but the expression of an impulse, sometimes present, sometimes remote, that is always urging the human impulse in the organization of such a society, so extensive in its membership, and in face of popular discouragements, especially that impalpable, but powerful resistance that society is always making to efforts of this kind, reveals the strength and foresight of its founders, and appeals to the good sense and interest of the public.

We all acknowledge the injustice that has delayed success to the effort woman has so long been making for the proper and definite adjustment of her position relative to the affairs of life; a delay which her insight and patience and perserverance has turned into a not unmixed evil. This very delay has, in many instances, led and even forced her into unobtrusive lines of development; to direct her energies to improvement in little and hidden ways, and to the application of her fine moral distinctions, to the solution of those problems which touch so profoundly, the home, and the welfare of society, all of which is tending, fortunately to prepare, not only herself, but also the public mind, for that active and equal cooperation which will, in time, naturally and inevitably devolve upon her. Woman's sagacity in these respects is illustrated in a thousand instances. It is amply illustrated in the selection, for special activity in this Woman's League of the three departments of Woman in Education—Woman in the Professions, and Woman in the Law.

*The very name League* as adopted by this ass[ociation] expresses a determination to join in close alliance for a definite purpose—in this case, the conservation and elevation of society. Could fifteen minutes be daily given to the quiet contemplation of what woman is accomplishing in this direction, it would banish many discouragements and rouse to renewed activity, that would demonstrate beyond cavil, not only her general ability, but her possession of a wisdom in practical affairs, supposed to be the peculiar prerogative of man.

She is earning a recognition of this wisdom, very surely in her success in the educational movement, in prison reform, and in sanitary matters.

In the great and busy city of Chicago, it is a woman who is solving the garbage question, clearing the tainted atmosphere and banishing infectious diseases by establishment of pure and healthful conditions.

Ever since George Washington and Betsy Ross put their heads together to evolve old glory, woman has been doing her part in lifting the nation up towards all Old Glory ought to signify, and when, the other day, under the alluring influence of many banners and martial music, and the seductions of good comradeship, our youth were beguiled into joining in the apotheosis of treason, it was woman's voice with man's that vainly essayed to recall public conscience to the duty of maintaining its honor.

We are a young people. Hitherto, in common life our energies have been absorbed in consideration of wherewithal shall we be schooled and clothed and fed. But now we are beginning to philosophize; to consider the relation of cause to effect of pure air and sunshine to a cleanly life, that a vicious man cannot make a good citizen, that out of our alleys and festering courts comes the seed of our prisons and jails. Would that the women of Washington would unite as one to eliminate these alley ways, breeders of disease, and moral death, shielded continuously behind the fine houses of the West End. Still public sanitation is not escaping woman's attention. To the Women's Law Class of 1887 New York City offered a prize essay on what women have accomplished for the protection of public health, and it may be that to woman's activity, we of the city of Washington will yet be indebted for the elimination of many nuisances and for reclaiming the broad, choked miasmatic section of the eastern branch of the Potomac.

There is another department of public health interest in which it may be that this Woman's League may serve the ends of both humanity and justice—the Police Court of our city. It is our duty as workers for public morality to look over carefully the Police Court records that we may know for what reason and in what manner the long list of offenders are compelled to appear in court. Women can not read these reports without observing with what alacrity our brave preservers of the public peace snatch up any little boys and poor homeless men and women, and present them promptly at court.

By what perversity of justice does it happen that the taking of a human life by the rich and thoughtless is made the occasion of excessive solicitude and leniency on the part of officials, while the sinking down upon the sidewalk of a worn out old man and the innocent picking of a few magnolia blossoms by an ignorant child are promptly made the occasion of arrest and detention? Such inequalities of justice turn the hearts of the poor against the administration of law and create in their minds the impression that its province is to protect the interests of the rich, but not those of the poor. We need not only Police Matrons but a woman as Associate Judge of the Police Court, and as warden of the woman's department at the jail.

This Woman's League is organized under conditions far more favorable to both free and concerted action than was ever before presented. To what one institution is she advancing, what shall I say? The grand old words of freedom and equality wound the supersensitive ear of conservatism, and arouse prejudice. I will say advancement—the advancing advancement of woman, the advance greatly due? To the bicycle! The effect of this beautiful exercise in freeing woman from mental restrictions and all unexpectedly bringing her onto a broader plain, not only of physical, but of intellectual and moral being, is well worth the study of moralists as illustrating how much more effective, as an agent of reform, is the wheel than argument, and alas also of how much more susceptible is poor human nature to an argument addressed to its self interest than to its reason alone. Mrs. Jonas Miller might have urged her health dress upon the public for a hundred years, and accomplished less than the bicycle is doing in as many months. Only the other day when a N.Y. newspaper sent inquiries to the principal hotels and restaurants in the city of New York, asking if they would admit women in Bloomer costume, most of them replied that they would admit them. What did this? The Bicycle. It is not so many years, however, but that many of us can remember, since in the streets of this city appeared a modest tricycle propelled by a woman. Women were shocked, men disgusted, and the small boys followed in companies jeering

& hooting, while the daily press caricatured in the most ridiculous manner the tricycle and its rider.

There is one department of education that deeply concerns every loyal Loyal League in our land and every loyal community and individual, the careful training of our children and youth in the duties that lead to good citizenship. We have hitherto been extremely careless in this matter, taking it for granted that our growing young Republic could make good citizens out of the most ill trained material, but we are learning that those who in childhood are trained to pay no respect to parents, the property or the rights of others, will scarcely in manhood, pay due respect to law, prove proper custodians of the public revenues, or legislate honestly for the good of the public.

Therefore, the women of Philadelphia, moved by these or similar considerations, are to organize the school children of the city into a "League of Good Citizenship." Let the mothers and teachers of our country have a care. Our children must be trained in civic virtue and in loyalty. Columbia has once nursed a viper in her bosom. Let her not do it a second time.

It has been asserted that the school books of the South fail to inculcate these virtues, and it has been asserted and denied that in Georgia the books forced by the state upon the colored schools, also offend the self respect of the colored people, and that they have no redress. This not a hidden danger. Are our public school educators sleeping that this subject does not stir them?

Where is the spirit of loyalty in our land, that it is not aroused to the necessity of securing to our Republic, the right education of its children, so that instead of lawlessness that like an engulfing wave has swept up from the South, till it seizes its victims within the very shadow of our Capitol, there shall abide loyalty, obedience to law and order, and the progress that follows the exercise of these virtues.

*Ms.*, Frederick Douglass Papers, Library of Congress,
Manuscripts Division, Washington, D.C.

## WOMAN SUFFRAGE
## (UNDATED SPEECH)

Ladies and gentlemen:
It is long since it was my privilege to address a convention of re-

formers in Boston. In my more youthful days, when slavery was the giant evil of the land, and demanded the voice and vote of the humblest for its removal, it was often my lot to be a speaker upon such occasion. But since the abolition of slavery, both my occupation and my facility as a speaker have sensibly diminished.

Yet I can truly say that it gives me very great pleasure to be again in Boston and to stand upon this platform, and to say my word, however humbly and unskillfully it may be, for the cause of woman.

When invited to be here I was compelled to comply for two reasons; first, because I believe in the justice of the cause of woman, and second, because I gratefully appreciate the services rendered by her to the cause of Emancipation.

When I consider what was done for the slave by such women as Lucretia Mott, Lydia Maria Child,[67] Elizabeth Cady Stanton, Maria W. Chapman,[68] Lucy Stone, Abby Kelley Foster, Angelina Grimké, Elizabeth Chace[69] and other noble women, I not only feel it a grateful duty, but a high privilege to give my voice and vote in favor of a larger sphere and broader liberty for the activities of woman.

I, however, come before you with little confidence in my ability to assist your cause. I can add nothing to the force and very little to the volume of argument in favor of the claims you make. The most I can hope to do is to give back to you in some humble measure the thought and feeling common to all the friends of this movement.

As in the days of the Antislavery conflict, so in respect of this cause, our mission is, the *reiteration* of truth familiar to all, for here as elsewhere there is nothing new under the sun. The terms new and old do not properly apply to any great truth or principle. Error may be new, or it may be old. It has a beginning and must have an end. But truth is neither new nor old. It is the fundamental law of the universe. It is upon this broad, unchangeable and eternal foundation, that every right of man or woman is based, and I know of no cause which rests more squarely upon this foundation than the cause which this convention has assembled to promote.

I congratulate you, my friends, upon the progress already made in fixing this idea of the equal rights of woman in the public mind and heart of this county. I think a glance at the history of your movement is full of encouragement. Though small and apparently insignificant in its origin, though limited in its resources, at the beginning met by the storm of derision and threatened with extinction, though the powers that be, in church and state, opposed it, though the heathen raged and the people imagined a vain thing, its growth has been strong, steady, and irrepressible. Those who doubt the ultimate success of this cause will do well to remember, not merely what remains to be done, but what has already been accomplished.

Forty years ago, woman was but feebly recognized as a factor in the political civilization of our country. She was almost unknown to the world as a platform and public teacher. Her silence in this field was akin to that of the grave. When she attempted to speak she started at the sound of her own voice. Her mission was to be seen but not heard. We have no better evidence of her progress, than is found in her complete triumph over this childlike timidity. I live in Washington and often listen to speeches in Congress, but the most eloquent and able speakers in Congress to day, do not speak with more self possession or assurance of fitness than such women as Mrs. Livermore,[70] Mrs. Stone, Mrs. Stanton, Miss Eastman and others. I am wrong however in asserting that woman was entirely silent in public forty years ago. She in fact made a good deal of noise more than twice forty years ago, and the fact shows the inconsistency of the opposition still felt to her speaking in public. Her voice was then louder in song than it is now in speech. Even the disciples of Paul would permit her to sing in the church, and would applaud her in the concert room, and on the boards of the theatre. Her voice was never dreadful or shocking, until it was made to express her own convictions of truth and duty.

A vast and wonderful change has taken place in the public mind as to what is proper for woman in this respect. In her right of speech her victory is complete. There is literally no language or speech in which her voice is not heard. In Europe as well as in America thousands listen to her eloquence and applaud her wisdom. She is hailed to day not only as an angel of beauty, but as an angel of peace, temperance, and social order.

Of course this victory has not come without effort and all at once. It has come gradually and in accordance with the Law of Evolution. It was in Scripture Phrase: "First the blade, then the ear, then the full corn in the ear." The boldest women in this movement did not think it wise at first to demand the right of suffrage. They came up to this as the last battle in their campaign for perfect freedom.

What they wanted first of all and most of all, at the beginning, was that great right, the most sacred of all rights, the right to think, and to freely utter their thoughts. They had pent up in their newly awakened souls message, a fiery protest against the social fetters into which bigotry, superstition and time honored custom had bound them for ages. This protest to the common ear was heard by men with astonishment. It was to them a wild and threatening cry of revolt, a shout of defiance from the barricades of rebellion surrounding the forts and arsenals of conservatism and social order, to unconditional surrender or fight. It signalled the uprising of one half of the human world against the established opinions of the other half, and that half not what is commonly called the better half. There is no question that if the demands of woman are complied with to the full extent to which she has been pleased to make them, we shall see a revolution, the most strange, radical and stupendous that the world has ever witnessed. It would equal and surpass that great struggle under Martin Luther for religious liberty.

At the beginning of this grand crusade, only a few women dared to stand forward and show their hand. It required a vast amount of conscience and surpassing courage to do so, but there were women equal to the occasion. Abby Kelley, Lucretia Mott, Sarah and Angeline Grimké were found worthy to espouse the cause in the dark day of its history, and it is good to remember their names, now that the cause has come into its Glory. Against popular usage, against prejudice, against church, state, press, pulpit, platform and the noisy tumult and abuse of the crowd, they rose in grandeur and glory alike the rainbow over the howling storm.

It is said that this movement cannot succeed, that woman can never be enfranchised. I do not say that she can. It is not necessary to the perfection of this paper to affirm that she can, and yet in view of the wonders of the age, he is a bolder man than I am, who affirms that she can not.

In judging of the possible success of this cause, we shall do well, not to measure its progress by the great distance at which it seems now to stand from its ultimate aim and object, or by the stupendous obstacles it has yet to overcome, but rather from the point way back in the past, from which it started, and by the tremendous obstacles it has already surmounted.

Woman has already secured a vast vantage ground. Her voice

and pen are both free. Archimedes only wanted a place for the fulcrum of his lever in order to move the world. Woman has found
the place in her ability to speak, write, publish, organize and agitate. She has in this a weapon superior to swords, guns, or dynamite. No man even now, running for Congress or the presidency or
any other office, wants to have the voice of the women against him.

See how wisely she has conducted this movement, how guarded
have been all her approaches to the vast citadel she has determined
to storm and capture. Her first demand was not for suffrage, but
for the right of speech. Her next was for higher education, and her
next was for an enlargement of her opportunities for making an
honest living. She has measurably compelled compliance with all
of these demands. She has found her way into colleges and universities, and greatly enlarged the boundaries of her industrial avocations. Forty years ago there were not thirty occupations open to
women. Now there are more than three hundred. Forty years ago
there were no colleges open, now there are none where she cannot
enter. Woman knew the potency of the cry for bread, and she sent
forth this terrible alarm—from all the destitute and miserable abodes
of her sex; from dark cellars, from dilapidated garrets, from fireless
hearthstones, from the helpless and desolate of every quarter where
glasseyed hunger extended its famished hand for bread! and that
cry as I have said has become measurably heeded.

Victor Hugo has said many true and touching things of the miseries
of man, but he has never said anything truer or more touching than
this: "He who has seen the misery of man only has seen nothing:
he must see the misery of woman: He who has seen the misery of
woman only has seen nothing: he must see the misery of children."
To man there are a thousand ways of escape to one for woman.

If this movement in behalf of woman had accomplished nothing
more than the enlargements of woman industrial pursuits, it would
have fully vindicated its right to be gratefully recognized as one of
the most beneficent movements of the age. It has increased the
number and variety, the worth and volume of woman's work and
usefulness in the world.

Nor will the good work in this direction cease to grow. The age is
one of discovery and invention: The grosser forms of labor are
being done by machinery—as this proceeds, and mind rather than
muscle shall be demanded for carrying on the work of the world—

woman will come in for a larger share of the work than is now her portion. The time is coming when even prejudice and superstition will have to admit that woman should do any thing and every thing that she can do and do well.

But now I come to the point, and that is the great and all commanding claim now set up by woman; the equal right to vote, the equal participation with man in the Government under which she lives. In this demand of the ballot, she, more than in all her other demands, shocks the nerves of her fellow citizens. It is a comprehensive and sweeping demand. It includes all that has gone before and all that can come after, even to holding the highest office in the Gift of the nation, for when woman shall vote woman will hold office. It means absolute, complete and perfect citizenship, with all that citizenship involves. It means the Ballot Box, the Jury Box, the cartridge Box and the knowledge Box, and an equal share in them all for woman! Already you are appalled at the magnitude of the claim and have pronounced it absurd and monstrous, but tarry a little and see if there be not reasonable ground for its support.

Who and what then is woman? Is there anything in her nature and condition which unfit her for the profession of the election franchise? Is she rational and intelligent being? Does she know right from wrong and good from evil? Is she a legitimate and proper subject of government? Is she capable of forming an intelligent opinion of public men and public measure, and may she in words express such opinions? Has she a *will* as well as a *mind?* Has she interests like those of men which may be promoted or hindered by legislation, administration, and judicial proceedings?

If these and similar questions are answered in the affirmative, as they must be, it does not appear after all that the claims woman sets up for the right to vote is in any sense unnatural, absurd or monstrous.

The more the subject is examined in the light of reason and in freedom from prejudice, the more it will appear that the right of woman to participate in the Government, stands upon the same bases as that which supports the claim of man to that great right or privilege.

If he is a subject of Government, so is she. If he has a mind, so has she. If he has interests to guard and protect, so has she. If he has a natural right to vote, so has she. She cannot rightfully exclude him, nor can he rightfully exclude her, and either to exclude the other is wrong, oppression, and usurpation.

If we turn to the constructive elements of the American Government, we are conducted to the same conclusion. The American doctrine of Liberty, is that governments derive their right to govern from the just consent of the governed, and declares that taxation without representation is tyranny, and the founders of the Republic went so far as to say that resistance to tyrants is obedience to God. On these principles woman no less than man has a right to vote. She has all the attributes that fit her for citizenship and a voter. Equally with man she is a subject of the law. Equally with man she is bound to know the law. Equally with man she is bound to obey the law. There is no more escape from its penalties for her than for him. When she commits crimes or violates the Law in any way, she is arrested, arraigned, tried, condemned, imprisoned like any other felon. Her womanhood does not excuse her from condign punishments. The Law takes no thought of her sex when she is accused of crime. Why should it take thought of her sex when bestowing its privileges?

Plainly enough woman has a positive grievance. She is taxed without representation, tried without a jury of her Peers, governed without her consent, punished for violating laws she has had no hand in making. She may well enough ask as she does ask: *Is this right?* She may go still further and denounce this arrangement as a conspiracy against her, at once disgraceful, unjust and unmanly on the part of the stronger sex.

If it be contended that government has a right to high intelligence for its direction, woman has that required qualification. There is no branch of knowledge which man has mastered that she may not master. She is seen in all the learned professions. She is teacher, preacher, doctor, lawyer—why may she not be a voter & statesman.

When the colored man was denied the right to vote because he did not know enough, I used to say: If he knows enough to know the law he knows enough to vote; if he knows as much when sober as an Irishman knows when drunk, he knows enough to vote, and so I can now say of woman.

Now after all, what argument can be brought against the conclusions thus reached? Is there anything in nature, reason, justice, or expedience against the right or propriety of extending suffrage to woman?

Yes: I hear this objection. It is said that woman is already represented in the Government; that she is represented by her husband, her sons, her brothers, and her parents. On first blush this objection seems valid, but in point of fact is it so? To the mind of a candid man, there is a fatal defect in this argument. It does not cover the ground it seems to cover, and is neither conclusive nor satisfactory. No man can be said to represent another person unless appointed by that person to do so. In the old times it was said that the rich represented the poor, and the whites represented the blacks, but neither the poor nor the blacks felt themselves represented, for neither had selected these to represent them. Besides, these self constituted represented themselves and their own interests, rather than those they pretended to represent. There is a wise proverb, "That those who have the cross will bless themselves." The same is true of the ballot. Give woman the ballot and she will represent herself or appoint some one who will faithfully represent her—some one who will be responsible to her for the use of the power she may confer upon him.

Then again, it is a fair question whether any man can properly represent a woman. It is about as much as man can do to represent himself. The great fact underlying the woman suffrage movement is this: *Woman is woman. She is herself*, and nobody else than herself. Her selfhood is as complete, perfect and absolute as is the selfhood of man. She cannot part with her personality any more than she can part with her identity. She can neither represent man nor can man represent woman.   This fundamental, unchangeable and everlasting condition of the fitness of things, is not only recognized by the law, but is organized into law and practice. Even in the relation of husband and wife, the individuality of the wife is preserved. Where the sale or transfer of property is concerned, the woman is consulted separate and apart from her husband. However united in feeling and interests they may be, the law recognizes and treats them as two separate individual persons, two minds, two wills, and each will equally entitled to be consulted independently of the other.

With this fundamental principle supported by reason as well as by law, the advocate of woman suffrage may advance to another

principle, quite as familiar, and self evident as the selfhood of woman—namely, the whole of a thing is more than a part, and this is
as true of humanity and of human powers as of anything else. The
whole people are more than a part of the people. All the men and
women together are more than all women by themselves or all the
men by themselves. Hence the combined wisdom and virtue of the
whole is more than the combined wisdom and virtue of a part. It
follows therefore that that government is strongest and best which
embodies the most wisdom and virtue.

A government by man alone is at best only a half supplied government. It is like a bird with only one wing—floundering to earth
unable to soar and loft to the highest and best. It is a maimed government, deprived of one half of the wisdom and goodness within
its reach. It is divested of woman's instructive perception of character and her quick sense of right and wrong, her tender solicitude for
childhood, and her abhorrence of war. It deprives itself her delicacy
and refinements, and makes possible drunken and dissolute rulers.

But I come to another far more popular objection to the enfranchisement of woman than the fact that she is said to be represented
by men. It is this:

"Suffrage will degrade woman. It will drag her down from her
present elevated position and plunge her into the muddy waters of
politics." Here are two objections chained together, and possibly
one is about as unsound as the other. As to the first it may be asked
what degradation can there be in placing woman on a platform of
political equality with man? Is man degraded by making him a voter?
You will say of course not. It makes him a ruler. He shares the honor,
power and dignity of the government, and what it does for him,
that it will do for woman. She may well say welcome to me is all
degradation that will make me the political equal of my husband,
father and brothers. To invest her with political rights, to consult
her as to the kind and quality of the men who shall make the laws,
and administer them, is not to degrade woman, but to elevate her
and increase her consequence as a member of society.

But, she is to be plunged (that's the word) into the muddy waters
of politics. She is not to step into, but to be plunged into the muddy
waters, that is she is to be covered all over with this muddy water.
Woman might well enough shrink from this plunge, and if it were
necessary, this "mud." What is politics any how? It is the science of

government. Now in science as in religion, to the pure all things are pure. This is as true in politics as in any thing else. There is no mud in politics other than that imported there by each individual, and the mud only touches those who carry it there. Whatever of *mud* and meanness you find there has this origin. The impurity is purely personal. Woman's presence at the polls would in my judgment do much to remove this reproach from American politics. She is the admitted conservator of manners, morals and decency.

But admitting this fact says the objector, it cannot be denied that politics will bring woman to the polls in uncomfortable contact with low, vulgar and coarse men. This objection is easily answered. Rather than violate principle of justice and fair play by denying woman the right to vote, let woman have a separate box in which to deposit her ballot and thereby avoid the unpleasant contact with vulgar men.

But are we not over nice, in fact more nice than wise in this solicitude for the protection of woman? Does the danger justify the alarm and apprehension? Is woman an entire stranger to the vulgar crowd? The facts show the contrary. She meets the crowd in the depot, in the market place, in the street car, in the theatre, in the church, on the rail road, and yet in all these places, she preserves her dignity and is uncontaminated. If this be true, and no one can well deny it, why may she not do the same thing at the polls where she only has to walk away—just as she takes a letter from the Post Office and returns it to her home?

Then again, will not the presence of woman at the polls produce the same effect there as elsewhere? Has not experience abundantly proven that the presence of woman is the best guarantee for order, decency and politeness every where? Two men may drop their respective votes in the same ballot box, but yet as a character and dignity be as wide asunder as the poles of the moral universe.

If seclusion, absence of contact with the outside world wins the best protection to womanly dignity, the harem would surpass the home. The women of the East, though caged, veiled and cushioned, not allowed to be seen by the vulgar crowd, and watched over by eyes as vigilant as the suspicions of despotism, are no purer than our American women. If the stories of travelers be true, they are far less so. Enforced morality is artificial morality. It is saved from drowning because it can find no water, and never learns to swim.

But there is another objection which a faithful discussion of this subject compels me to notice. It is this. It is alleged that woman herself is opposed to the woman suffrage movement. That she is contented and happy and is extremely satisfied with her condition, and would not have the ballot if it were given to her by a change in the Constitution.

There is doubtless some truth in this statement, but it is manifestly not the truth and the whole truth and nothing but the truth.

If the opponents of woman suffrage really believed in the truth of what they say on this point, they would not be at the pains and expense of writing long arguments, making long speeches, and preaching long sermons against the woman suffrage movement. They would allow it to fall by its own weight and weakness.

But is it true that woman is so contented with her present condition and would not have the ballot if it were given her? It is a statement which may be fairly questioned. Years ago I heard the same argument employed against the Abolition movement. The slaves were then the contented and happy people who would not have their Liberty if it were given them, just as we are now told that women are contented and happy and would not have the ballot if it were given them. It was not true of the slaves then and it is not true of women now. The same men who told us of the contentment and happiness of the slaves were busy at the same time framing laws to prevent their escape from slavery. When men say one thing and (do) another and opposite thing men generally discredit the former and believe the latter on the principle that example is better than precept.

It must be admitted that this argument does not dispose of the objection conclusively. It does not follow that because the slave was not contented and happy in slavery that women are not contented in their condition. Nor does it follow that because the slave wanted his freedom, that women want to vote. What I have said simply proves the probability of what is true.

But what after all, if it could be shown that women generally do not want to vote. That fact would only be binding on them. It would not affect the right of those who do want to vote. Because one man does not want freedom is no reason why another should be made a slave.

It is for men to recognize the right of woman to vote, and leave woman the option as they leave man the option whether they shall vote or not. When they do that it will be time enough for them to state what woman will or will not do.

Should the right be once acknowledged, and I venture to say that no President could ever be elected to that high office without the votes by women. The most persuasive eloquence of both parties would be employed upon them. Men who opposed granting suffrage would not be behind those who favored it in soliciting the support of the women voters of the country.

But here is another objection, one very much relied upon, in opposition to the extension of suffrage to woman. She can not perform military service. She is physically incapable of bearing arms and can not therefore fight battles of the country. This objection which seems so strong to those who bring it, contains a vice and a weakness even more fatal to its validity than the objection just disposed of. It sets one of the grandest rights of human nature upon a purely physical basis. According to this the basis of civil government is not mind but matter, not reason but force, not right but might, not human but bestial. It belongs to man rather as a savage than to man as a civilized being. If this theory of government were sound, Sullivan the Slugger should have more political power than Sherman the Senator. The burley prize fighter should stand higher than the President. It is a doctrine which rules out nearly all the great men of the world, for  the profoundest thinkers and students are generally more distinguished for mind than for muscle. If those only who are strong enough to defend the country on the battlefield should be allowed to vote, one third of all the men of this country would be disfranchised. All men over forty years of age, and all who have bodily ailments, are exempted from military service, yet all such men have the right and do vote. The denial of woman's right on the ground of physical disability, appears not only wrong but mean, since it is a discrimination against her which is not applied to others.

But it is not true that all women cannot perform military duty. History affords the contrary. There is no more thrilling chapter in the history of the reformation than that which describes the defense of Leyden where wives fought beside their husbands, sisters by the sides of their brothers and where the women were as brave and enduring as the men. In our late war she did important military service in her care for the sick and wounded, in her administrative capacity, in the gathering and distribution of supplies, in the establishment and support of hospitals and even in the planning of campaigns.

But granting all that is claimed as to woman's unfitness to perform military duty. Is not war exceptional and peace the normal condition of society? Shall we base a right upon the exception, and disregard the principle? Is that logical and reasonable? What right have we to measure the rights of a human being under civil government, by a condition of things that excludes civil government. War sets aside civil government and brings it under martial law. Under it vice becomes virtue, stealing, lying and robbing excusable and murder meritorious. Surely ability to do these things should not be made the bases of civil or political rights.

But perhaps a more serious objection to woman's participation in civil government than either of the preceding ones relates to its supposed effect upon the home. It is alleged that woman suffrage will introduce strife and division into the family. It is said that woman will be ranged on one side and the man will be on the other, that the brother will be on one side and the sister on the other and that home will no longer be sweet home and that peace and tranquility will no longer dwell under the family roof.

No such consequences would be alarming if they were necessary or inevitable, but they do not appear to the eye of sober reason in any such light and may therefore be rejected. The objection assumes that differences of opinion in the state may be more safely tolerated than in the family which is bound together by respect, tenderness and love. It holds that in order to have peace and tranquility in the family, the woman, the wife, the daughter and the sister must have no opinions of their own, or at any rate must not be allowed to express such opinions if they have them, that they must deny their intellect and conscience and become moral, social and intellectual non entities, bodies without souls, in fact like the Gods of the heathen, having eyes and see not, and tongues and speak not.

Certainly a principle which requires such self stultification and self abasement cannot be sound or other than absurd and vicious. But happily upon enfranchisement of woman we have no right to predicate any such dire consequences. Husbands and wives differ in opinion, every day, about a variety of things and yet dwell together in love and harmony. How insufferably flat, stale and unprofitable is that family where no difference of opinion enters! Who on earth can want to spend his or her days as a simple echo?—a body without a soul, a mind without an opinion, a mere bundle of thoughtless concessions or light under a bushel, a talent buried in silence, a piece of intellectual emptiness and social nothingness? A difference of opinion, like a discord in music, sometimes gives the highest effects of harmony. A thousand times better is it to have a brave outspoken woman by our side than a piece of mincing nothingness as now described. For myself from what I know of the nature of the human understanding, I at once suspect the sincerity of the man or woman whᴖ never has an opinion in opposition to mine. Differing as human minds do in all their processes and operations, such uniform agreement is unnatural and must be false, assumed and dishonest. The peace of no family or state can rest upon any foundation less solid than truth and honesty.

But here comes another objection which is a point blank contradiction to the one just answered. It is a positive deꞏnial that any thing will be gained or lost in the final result of any election by the enfranchisement of woman: because it is affirmed that woman's vote will only express the views and wishes of her husband and brothers. In the former objection the home was to be broken up by disagreement, and in the second there is to be no disagreement. Woman will vote according to the political opinions of her husband, and hence there will be no difference except in the additional number of votes cast and counted. We have only to array one of these objections against the other to neutralize and destroy the effect of both. Both may be wrong, but both cannot be right.

But suppose however that the lattter objection is true, that is suppose that woman will vote the same tickets voted by her husband. It is plain in that case no more harm would result than from his single vote. The state would receive no detriment, and therefore the objection is groundless.

But while upon this reckoning no special good or ill would come to the state from woman's voting, the extension of suffrage to her would vastly augment her importance and dignity as a member of society. It would bring her into honorable relations with the government, and make her a full and complete citizen. No class of persons can be excluded from the government without injury, and no persons can be included without benefit. If woman is enfranchised, she will be consulted as to both the man and the measures of the government, and this will elevate her and add to her influence. If she can be thus advanced in her interests, without injury to the state, the privilege should not be denied her. Proscription is a bitter affliction to woman or man. It is the mark of Cain set upon him or her. In a government like ours, where the doctrine of universal suffrage prevails, for any one to be deprived of it is a positive hardship. What business have we to inflict this hardship upon sensitive woman? She is the moulder of manners, the model of refinement, the mainstay of virtue, and yet our laws class her with minor criminals and idiots, and like those declare she shall not vote.

In Europe where governments are based upon divine rights, where a few are born to rule and the many are subjects, this hardship of being denied a voice in the government is not so keenly felt, because the disability is borne by all. The divided burden makes the weight for each light, but here with us the case is different. To single out woman and class her with felons in the denial of suffrage is not only a hardship and a humiliation but an insult.

I have been laughed at for my views on this subject but I am not ashamed to say that I am ready to go with him or her who goes furthest in all reasonable efforts to remove this disability from woman, to blot out this handwriting of barbarism, and to place woman side by side with man as his equal before the law and in citizenship.

But here comes an objection which is beyond all other dangerous and difficult to deal with, because of its inclusiveness, vagueness and because it touches the Infinite side of human nature. It comes dressed in saintly robes, its voice is sepulcheral, and it speaks with pontifical authority without any appeal to reason. It meets us with the outstretched arms and the uplifted eyes of religion. It tells us that the woman suffrage movement tends to infidelity. This charge has one advantage other than its vagueness and that is its age. It is positively old. It has appeared in all of the world ages and has been met with by nearly every effort yet made to make the world wiser and better. It weakened on the shores of Jordan eighteen hundred years before it was heard on the shores of the Potomac. It was met by the fathers of this Republic when they declared that all men were created equal. It was heard by Garrison[71] when he denounced slaveholding as a crime and a slaveholding church as a synagogue of Satan. It was heard by Galileo when he discovered and declared the truth of the Diurnal motion of the earth. It was heard by Martin Luther when he denounced the abuses in the Roman church, and it is heard to day from the lips of those who despise their fellow men because of their color.

I think the woman suffrage people ought to thank Doctor Patton[72] for furnishing evidence of the justice of their claim to suffrage, by his refusing to attack in any direct way. He does not question the rightfulness of the claim, but only the assertion of the claim. This he thinks leads to Infidelity, & the proof of this allegation is that some of those who assert the claim have been Infidels. This kind of reasoning may do for a teacher of theology, but would be scouted from the court room if any one should be simple enough to bring it there. Can it be accepted that because the Devil once told the truth, that therefore the truth leads to the Devil?

Shall we say because infidels advocated the Declaration of Independence, that therefore the Declaration of Independence had infidel tendencies? Shall we say that because infidels advocated the Abolition of slavery, therefore the abolition movement had an infidel tendency? I have great respect for the President of Howard University but none for his reasoning upon the woman suffrage movement. According to his reasoning a bad man makes a good cause bad and should lead men to shun it. Otherwise why does he assail the advocates of a cause instead of the cause itself. The fact that he does not attack the principle of equal suffrage is evidence that he thinks it too well fortified by reason and justice, so he takes the back handed, I will not say underhanded way, of making his assault. Shall we say that because Mr. Ingersoll[73] admits colored men to his meetings, and evangelical workers do not, that therefore infidelity is right and Christianity is wrong? Would such reasoning suit the American people? Shall we praise infidelity and curse Christianity, because all infidels in this instance act like a Christian and a Christian acts like an infidel? No, no, let us rather say that every cause shall be tried by its own intrinsic merits, and not by the perfections and imperfections of its advocates. Suppose we should condemn the pulpit because we can point to scores of the clergy, who have committed crimes. I imagine that the pulpit would very soon detect the unsoundness of such reasoning. Until Doctor Patton can show us a thus saith the Lord that woman shall not vote, we may still be permitted to believe that the woman suffrage movement does not tend to infidelity.

*Ms.*, Frederick Douglass Papers, Library of Congress,
Manuscripts Division, Washington, D.C.

## NOTES

1. The Women's Association of Philadelphia was an interracial organization formed to obtain support for abolition and to improve the conditions of free blacks in the North.

2. The bloomer costume was a knee-length dress worn as a belted tunic over "turkist trousers" nipped in at the ankle. It was intended to give more freedom to women and was popularized by Mrs. Amelia J. Bloomer (1818-1894), editor of *The Lily*, which favored suffrage, temperance, and other reforms.

3. Mrs. Jane Grey Cannon Swisshelm (1815-1884) was one of the first women in America to publish her own newspaper. In 1847, she used a legacy from her mother to establish the *Pittsburgh Saturday Visiter [sic]*, a political and literary weekly that advocated abolition, temperance, and woman suffrage.

4. Clarina Irene Howard Nichols (1810-1885) took over financial and editorial control of her husband's paper, the *Windham County Democrat*, at Brattleboro after he became ill. She ran the paper from 1843 to 1853 and wrote many editorials in favor of woman's rights.

5. Antoinette Louisa Brown (1825-1921) joined the Congregational Church at the age of nine and was soon speaking publicly in meetings. She completed a literary course at Oberlin College in 1847 and a theological course in 1850. Refused a ministerial license because of her sex, she preached wherever churches would receive her until 1852 when she became the regular pastor of the Congregational Church in South Butler, New York. She was active in the abolition, temperance, and woman's rights movements. In January 1856, she married Dr. Samuel C. Blackwell, brother of Elizabeth and Henry Brown Blackwell.

6. The Liberty party was formed by abolitionists who broke from the nonvoting doctrine of William Lloyd Garrison, based themselves on the anti-slavery interpretation of the Constitution, and urged political action as one of the means of abolishing slavery. After he split with Garrison and Garrisonian abolitionism, Douglass became active in the Liberty party.

7. Thomas Wentworth Higginson (1823-1911) was an abolitionist and

woman suffrage advocate, a leader in the fight against the Fugitive Slave Act in Massachusetts, and a proponent of a free Kansas. He was colonel of the first colored regiment in the Civil War. In *Woman and Her Wishes,* Higginson ridiculed the arguments advanced against the rights of women.

8. William Henry Channing (1810-1884), nephew of William Ellery Channing, was a Unitarian minister, reformer, and woman's rights advocate.

9. Lucy Stone (1818-1893) was one of the foremost woman's rights advocates and active Abolitionists. She lectured extensively on woman's rights, anti-slavery, and temperance reform. In 1855, she married Henry Brown Blackwell, retaining her own name. People who did the same, or sympathized with the practice, were called "Lucy Stoners." She broke with Elizabeth Cady Stanton and Susan B. Anthony in 1869 and formed the American Woman Suffrage Association with Stanton as president, Anthony the National Woman Suffrage Association. The schism was healed later that same year when the two organizations merged to form the National American Woman Suffrage Associatin with Stanton as president, Anthony vice president, and Stone chairman of the executive committee.

10. *The Una* was published by Pauline Wright Davis. Established in February 1853, it was the first distinctively woman's rights paper published in the United States.

11. Harriet Kezia Hunt (1805-1875) was a pioneer woman physician and reformer. She began practicing medicine in 1835 but was refused entrance to Harvard Medical School in 1847 and 1850.

12. Paulina Wright Davis (1813-1876) was an early woman's rights advocate. She married Francis Wright, a merchant of wealth and position in Utica, New York, in 1833. After his death two years later, she spent much of her time in the anti-slavery cause and in studying anatomy and physiology. She started *The Una* in 1853, and later contributed to other woman's rights papers.

13. The Maine Law of 1851, sponsored by Neal Dow, the Maine prohibitionist and mayor of Portland, set the precedent for temperance legislation.

14. Elizabeth Cady Stanton (1815-1902) was the foremost figure in the nineteenth-century woman's rights movement. Born of a wealthy family, she married Henry B. Stanton in 1840 and joined with him in the abolitionist crusade. Both attended the World Anti-Slavery Convention in London, from which women were excluded. Mrs. Stanton was the prime force behind the Seneca Falls Convention of 1848, and with Susan B. Anthony devoted her time and energy to the woman's rights agitation. After the Civil War, she (with Anthony) was one of the editors of *The Revolution.* Mrs. Stanton organized the National Woman Suffrage Association and helped prepare the *History of Woman Suffrage.*

15. Susan B. Anthony (1820-1906) was a militant woman suffrage leader and an associate of Elizabeth Cady Stanton. She began her career as a school teacher, temperance advocate, and anti-slavery speaker during the 1850s, but devoted more and more time to woman's right to vote. She was one of the organizers of the National Woman Suffrage Association (1869), and, in 1872, she defied state statutes by attempting to vote. She was president of the National American Suffrage Association (1892-1900) and fought for a national woman suffrage amendment.

16. The reference is to Nancy Talbot Clark (1825-1901), pioneer woman physician in the United States.

17. The Hutchinson Family Singers were a regular feature at abolition and woman's rights meetings.

18. Douglass is referring to the fact that when Samuel Ringgold Ward, black abolitionist, lectured in the Second Presbyterian Church of Philadelphia—despite the fact that the notice for the meeting announced that "the lower Saloon will be appropriated exclusively to our white fellow citizens"— Douglass issued a special supplement to *The North Star* denouncing his friend's "shameful concession to the spirit of slavery and prejudice" (*The North Star*, May 30, 1850).

19. When Miss Elizabeth Greenfield, the "Black Swan," sang at concerts at which blacks were excluded, Douglass lashed out at her betrayal of her people. (See page 19). "She should be called no longer the *Black Swan* but the Black Raven," wrote Douglass (*The North Star*, February 26, 1852).

20. Louis Kossuth, the Hungarian patriot, Father Mathew, the Irish temperance leader, and John Mitchel, the Irish reformer, were all criticized in the anti-slavery press, including *The North Star*, for refusing to speak out against slavery while they were in the United States. The Free Church of Scotland (an organization based on the right of congregations to control the appointment of their own ministers) had sent a deputation to the United States in 1844 to form an alliance with churches in this country to solicit funds to build Free Churches and pay Free ministers in Scotland. An outburst of indignation arose from American abolitionists when the delegation raised funds from slaveholders and entered into alliance with southern churches. While in Scotland, Douglass spoke at many meetings demanding that the Free Church *"Send Back the Money."*

21. Charles L. Reason, a black abolitionist leader in Philadelphia, was one of those excluded from Mrs. Stone's lecture. It was his letter in *The North Star* of February 10, 1854, denouncing Mrs. Stone which caused Douglass's editorial comment.

22. Stephen Arnold Douglas (1813-1861), Illinois political leader, U.S. Senator (1847-1861), and advocate of the doctrine of popular sovereignty, was responsible for the Kansas-Nebraska Act of 1854. Douglas took part in

a series of debates on the question of slavery with Abraham Lincoln in 1858. In 1860, he was an unsuccessful candidate for President on the northern Democratic ticket.

23. Wendell Phillips (1811-1884) was one of the leading Garrisonian abolitionists, a great orator who fought persistently against slavery and for woman's rights before the Civil War, full freedom for blacks and the rights of labor after the war.

24. Parker Pillsbury (1809-1898) was a leading follower of William Lloyd Garrison and a close associate of Elizabeth Cady Stanton and Susan B. Anthony in the woman suffrage movement. He opposed granting suffrage to Negroes in the Fifteenth Amendment if women were not included.

25. Henry Brown Blackwell (1825-1909) was one of the earliest male advocates of woman suffrage. He married Lucy Stone on May 1, 1855, on which day they published a joint protest against the inequalities in the marriage law. A leading abolitionist, he wrote a message in 1867 to the southern legislatures proposing the extension of woman suffrage in the South as a counterbalance to Negro suffrage. Late in his life Blackwell became editor, without pay, of *The Woman's Journal.*

26. Charles Lenox Remond (1810-1873), son of a prosperous businessman in Salem, Massachusaetts, was the best known black abolitionist until the rise of Frederick Douglass. A delegate to the World Anti-Slavery Convention in London in 1840, he refused to take his seat because women delegates were excluded. Returning home after two years on the anti-slavery lecture circuit in Great Britain, he addressed Massachusetts legislators, convincing them to end segregation on the railroads of the state.

27. Frances Ellen Watkins Harper (1825-1911) was born free in Maryland and became a noted anti-slavery lecturer and writer. The author of ten volumes of poetry and a novel, *Iola Leroy,* she lectured and taught in the South after the Civil War. She was active in the woman's rights movement and was a founder of the National Association of Colored Women.

28. Originally used to express hatred and contempt of Indians, the word *Copperhead* was applied by northerners during the Civil War to northern sympathizers of the southern cause.

29. James Brooks (1810-1873), publisher of the pro-southern *New York Express* and Congressman from New York City in 1864, was a leading Democrat of the Copperhead type.

30. Samuel S. Cox (1824-1889), journalist and Congressman from Ohio, was one of the leading Copperheads in Congress and a friend of Clement L. Vallandigham, the leader of the Copperheads.

31. Anti-Negro riots broke out in Memphis and New Orleans during the spring and summer of 1866 in which scores of blacks and their white allies were killed or wounded.

The reference to the New York mobs is to the Draft Riots of 1863 during which wild mobs, while unleashing their hatred against the National Conscription Act, committed unspeakable atrocities against the black community, murdering or maiming any Negro they encountered.

32. Lucretia C. Mott (1793-1880) was one of the pioneer woman's rights advocates and one of the first women to speak in public. A minister of the Society of Friends, she was in the anti-slavery movement. With Elizabeth Cady Stanton she helped initiate the Seneca Falls Convention of 1848.

33. Theodore Tilton (1835-1907), famous editor of *The Independent* and the *Golden Age*, was a leading abolitionist and advocate of woman's rights. He became involved in the suit against Henry Ward Beecher for adultery, a case which filled newspapers from 1870 to 1875.

34. Henry Ward Beecher (1813-1887), popular preacher of the Plymouth Congregational Church in Brooklyn, roused sentiment against slavery and for woman's rights in sermons from the pulpit. His activity in sending guns to keep Kansas free following passage of the Kansas-Nebraska Act gave rise to the term *Beecher's Bibles*. After the Civil War, Beecher was a vocal opponent of working class movements. He gained wide notoriety in the scandal involving the wife of Theodore Tilton.

35. Horace Greeley (1811-1872) was the famous editor of the *New York Tribune* and supporter of Fourierist communities. He was the leading Republican spokesman until he broke with the party and ran for President on the Liberal-Republican ticket in 1872. He was overwhelmingly defeated by Ulysses S. Grant, the Republican candidate.

36. Olympia Brown (1835-1926) was the first woman in the United States to be ordained to the ministry of a regularly constituted ecclesiastical body. After graduating from the Theological School of St. Lawrence University at Canton, New York, in 1863, she was ordained in the same year to the ministry of the Universal Church. In 1866, she met Susan B. Anthony and became an ardent advocate of woman's rights.

37. The reference is to the impeachment proceedings against President Andrew Johnson initiated by the Radical Republicans in 1868 because of his opposition to Radical Reconstruction and his sympathy for the former slave-owners. Johnson was acquitted and served out his term as President.

38. George Francis Train (1829-1904), financier, speculator, and eccentric radical, was accused of having been a Copperhead during the Civil War. He helped finance *The Revolution* and wrote articles on the currency question for the paper.

39. Under the Fourteenth Amendment, a state's representation in the House of Representatives could be reduced proportionately as it excluded males over twenty-one years of age from voting because of race, color, or previous condition of servitude. This clause was planned as a warning to pressure states to extend suffrage to Negro males. But between 1868 and 1870, the only northern state that heeded the warning and enacted Negro

suffrage was Minnesota. As a result, blacks and their allies pushed for a Fifteenth Amendment.

Brown had campaigned in Kansas in 1867 in favor of a proposition submitted to the vote of the people to amend the state constitution by striking out the word "male."

40. Thaddeus Stevens (1792-1868) was an anti-slavery Whig who became a leading Republican spokesman for equality for blacks. During Reconstruction, as leader of the House of Representatives and of the Joint Committee of Reconstruction, he fought for a radical plan of Reconstruction which included Negro suffrage. He was buried, at his direction, in the Negro cemetery of Lancaster, Pennsylvania.

41. Under the Radical Republican plan of Reconstruction sponsored in the House by Thaddeus Stevens and in the Senate by Charles Sumner, southern states could be readmitted to the Union only if they extended suffrage to Negro males twenty-one years of age or over.

42. Josephine Sophie Griffing (1814-1872) was an early anti-slavery and woman's rights activist in Ohio. During the Civil War, she did immense work for the Loyal League, and after the war served as a paid agent of the National Freedmen's Relief Association of the District of Columbia. While she worked closely with leaders of the woman's suffrage movement, she did not share the views of many of the leaders that the Negro should not be enfranchised if white women were not. In 1867, Mrs. Griffing helped organize the Universal Franchise Association of the District of Columbia and became its president.

43. Earlier, Douglass had spoken briefly on a dispute between Reverend Stephen S. Foster and Elizabeth Cady Stanton. Reverend Foster opposed Mrs. Stanton as president of the association because, he charged, she had taken a stand in *The Revolution* against Negro rights, and had referred to that "infamous Fifteen Amendment," because it did not include suffrage for women. Douglass, in an effort to pour oil on the troubled waters, asserted that Foster had the right to make the charge and Stanton the right to answer it. "We are used to freedom of speech," he declared, "and there is a profound conviction in the minds of reformers in general, that error may be safely tolerated, while truth is left free to counteract it."

44. Julia Ward Howe (1819-1910), wife of Dr. Samuel G. Howe, became famous as the author of "Battle Hymn of the Republic." In her old age, Mrs. Howe became a leading advocate of woman's rights and an associate of Lucy Stone. She organized the New England Suffrage Association in 1868 and became its long-time president.

45. A slightly different version of this part of the speech appeared in *The Revolution* of May 20, 1869. In this version the following appears: "The old anti-slavery school and others have said that the women must stand back and wait until the other class shall be recognized. But we say

that if you will not give the whole loaf and justice and suffrage to an entire people, give it to the most intelligent first. (Applause.) If intelligence, justice, and morality are to be placed in the government, then let the question of woman be brought up first and that of the negro last. (Applause)."

The Revolution of May 20 and May 27, 1869 carried the speeches at the convention.

46. The Ku Klux Klan was a secret organization organized in the South to terrorize Negroes, prevent them from using their voting privileges, overthrow Radical Reconstruction, and restore white supremacy.

47. In the winter of 1870, forty women of Hyde Park, Massachusetts, walked through the snow to deposit their ballots in a separate box. But the Massachusetts legislature refused to recognize the validity of their votes.

48. The reference is to the Franco-Prussian War of 1870.

49. The split in the woman suffrage movement which took place in May 1869 led to the formation in Cleveland in November 1869 of the American Woman Suffrage Association and, later, of the Union Woman's Suffrage Association. The effort to reunite the woman's movement in 1870 was enthusiastically supported by Douglass.

50. Gerrit Smith (1797-1874) was a wealthy New York philanthropist who was at first a follower of William Lloyd Garrison and then became an outstanding political abolitionist. A close friend of Douglass and often his financial supporter, Smith played a leading role in various social reforms, including woman's rights.

51. Samuel J. May (1797-1871), a Unitarian minister, was a leader in the abolitionist, temperance, and woman's rights movements.

52. Charlotte B. Wilbour, a club leader and social reformer, lectured frequently on woman's rights.

53. Theodore Tilton was the editor of The Independent.

54. Charles Sumner (1811-1874), leading anti-slavery Senator from Massachusetts, was assaulted on the Senate floor following his speech on "The Crime Against Kansas." Sumner stood firmly for equality for Negroes and fought for a Radical Reconstruction program after the Civil War.

55. The argument is reminiscent of that advanced by the Liberty party and other political abolitionists that the Constitution was inherently antislavery, a position Douglass firmly espoused following his split with the Garrisonians.

56. Victoria Woodhull (1838-1927) was an advocate of woman's rights and labor reform and was a member of Section 12 of the First International in the United States. Together with her sister Tennessee Claflin, she became a speculator in Wall Street, founded Woodhull & Claflin's Weekly, and became notorious as an advocate of free love. She was nominated for President on the Equal Rights ticket in 1872 at a convention in New York City which also nominated Douglass as its vice-presidential candidate. She and

sister left for England in the late 1870s where both married into wealthy families.

57. Celia Logan (1840-1904) later became a well-known American author.

58. Henry Clay (1777-1852), Senator from Kentucky and U.S. Secretary of State, was noted as the author of the Compromise of 1850. Clay also played a leading role in the Missouri Compromise of 1820.

59. On September 15, 1886, Douglass and his second wife, Helen Pitts Douglass, left the United States for a trip which covered Europe and Egypt.

60. The International Council of Woman was organized in 1888 as a federation of existing women's organizations. Its first president was Frances Willard, the temperance and woman's rights advocate.

61. Theodore Parker (1810-1860), religious liberal and scholar, became a leading abolitionist and one of the fiercest opponents of the Fugitive Slave Act of 1850.

62. Douglass delivered another brief speech at the meeting in which he paid tribute to Theodore D. Weld, the famous abolitionist, Clara Barton, founder of the American Red Cross, and Samuel Sewall, who had helped fugitive slaves. All three were at the meeting, and Douglass expressed the hope that they would address the delegates.

63. The Bethel Literary Society was the leading Negro organization in Washington, D.C. Douglass lectured frequently to the society, especially in commemoration of the abolition of slavery in the District of Columbia.

64. The famous Grimké sisters, Sarah and Angelina, were born in a distinguished South Carolina family, became Quakers, and, because of their anti-slavery views, were forced to leave for the North in 1836. They were among the first women to speak in public against slavery and became distinguished in the anti-slavery and woman's rights movements. Angelina Grimké married Theodore D. Weld.

65. Abigail Kelley Foster (1810-1887), a Quaker teacher, abandoned her teaching in 1837 for the anti-slavery lecture platform and soon became one of the most militant figures in the abolitionist movement. After 1850, she became prominent in the woman's rights movement along with her husband, Stephen S. Foster. She did not agree with Douglass on a number of issues, especially because of his split with Garrison, but their cool relations changed in the later years of her life.

66. Victor Marie Hugo (1802-1885), French author of novels, plays, and poetry and leader of the romantic movement, was an outstanding spokesman for social reform. Douglass honored Hugo for his effort to save John Brown from the gallows and for speaking out in favor of the abolition of slavery in Martinique and Guadaloupe.

67. Lydia Maria Child (1802-1880) was associated more with anti-slavery than with woman's rights. As an anti-slavery writer and speaker, she was among the greatest. A popular writer, she was the author of *An Appeal in*

*Favor of That Class of Americans Called Africans* (1833) and edited the pro-Garrisonian *National Anti-Slavery Standard.*

68. Maria Weston Chapman (1806-1885) was the driving force behind the Boston Female Anti-Slavery Society and edited Garrison's *Liberator* for periods when he was ill. The poet James Russell Lowell called Chapman "the coiled-up mainspring of the anti-slavery movement." Early in his career in the anti-slavery movement, Douglass resented Chapman's patronizing attitude towards him and fought for his right to be independent.

69. Elizabeth Buffum Chace (1806-1899), the vigorous anti-slavery advocate in Rhode Island, resigned from the Society of Friends in 1843 because she felt it too indifferent to the slavery question. She entertained Douglass at her home whenever he visited Rhode Island. Chace was one of the sponsors of the Woman's Rights Convention held in Worcester, Massachusetts, in 1850.

70. Mary Ashton Rice Livermore (1820-1905), Illinois reformer and suffragist, was elected president of the Illinois Woman's Suffrage Association and published *The Agitator* in the cause of woman's suffrage.

71. William Lloyd Garrison (1803-1879) organized the movement for "immediate emancipation." He maintained the battle against slavery through his journal, *The Liberator*, issued from January 1, 1831, to the end of 1865, and through the American Anti-Slavery Society which he organized in 1833. He was a national leader in the fight for woman's equality. Douglass was his close associate until the two split over the questions of political action and "moral suasion" as the major method in combatting slavery.

72. William D. Patton, president of Howard University, delivered a public attack on woman suffrage in Washington, charging that it would encourage infidelity. The use of the word *infidelity* in the controversy involved its religious connotation.

73. Robert G. Ingersoll (1833-1899) was a lawyer, attorney-general of Illinois, and leading Republican spokesman. His shocking lectures depicting the Bible as a tissue of falsehoods made him known as "the Great Agnostic."

# 2      TRIBUTES TO WOMEN

## A GALLERY OF ANTI-SLAVERY WOMEN

I shall never forget the first time I ever saw and heard Lucretia Mott. It was in the town of Lynn, Massachusetts. It was not in a magnificent hall, where such as she seemed to belong, but in a little hall, over Jonathan Buffum's store, the only place then open, even in that so-called radical anti-slavery town, for an anti-slavery meeting on Sunday. But in this day of small things, the smallness of the place was no matter of complaint or murmuring. It was a cause of rejoicing that any kind of place could be had for such a purpose. But Jonathan Buffum's courage was equal to this and more.

The speaker was attired in the usual Quaker-dress, free from startling colors, plain, rich, elegant, and without superfluity—the very sight of her a sermon. In a few moments after she began to speak, I saw before me no more a woman, but a glorified presence, bearing a message of light and love from the Infinite to a benighted and strangely wandering world, straying from the paths of truth and justice into the wilderness of pride and selfishness, where peace is lost and true happiness is sought in vain. I heard Mrs. Mott thus, when she was comparatively young. I have often heard her since, sometimes in the solemn temple, and sometimes under the open sky, but whenever and wherever I have listened to her, my heart was always made better, and my spirit raised by her words; and in speaking thus for myself I am sure I am expressing the experience of thousands.

Kindred in spirit with Mrs. Mott was Lydia Maria Child. They both exerted an influence with a class of the American people which neither Garrison, Phillips, nor Gerrit Smith could reach. Sympathetic in her nature, it was easy for her to "remember those in bonds as bound with them;" and her "appeal for that class of Americans called Africans," issued, as it was, at an early stage in the anti-slavery conflict, was one of the most effective agencies in arousing attention to the cruelty and injustice of slavery. When with her husband, David Lee Child, she edited the *National Anti-Slavery Standard*, that paper was made attractive to a broad circle of readers from the circumstance that each issue contained a "Letter from New York," written by her on some passing subject of the day, in which she always managed to infuse a spirit of brotherly love and good will, with an abhorrence of all that was unjust, selfish, and mean, and in this way won many hearts to anti-slavery who else would have remained cold and indifferent.

Of Sarah and Angelina Grimké I knew but little personally. These brave sisters from Charleston, South Carolina, had inherited slaves, but in their conversion from Episcopacy to Quakerism, in 1828, became convinced that they had no right to such inheritance. They emancipated their slaves and came North and entered at once upon the pioneer work in the advancing education of woman, though they saw then in the course only their duty to the slave. They had "fought the good fight" before I came into the ranks, but by their unflinching testimony and unwavering courage, they had opened the way and made it possible, if not easy, for other women to follow their example.

It is memorable of them that their public advocacy of anti-slavery was made the occasion of the issuing of a papal bull, in the form of a "pastoral letter," by the evangelical clergy of Boston, in which the churches and all God-fearing people were warned against their influence.

For solid, persistent, indefatigable work for the slave Abby Kelley was without a rival. In the *History of Woman Suffrage* just published by Mrs. Stanton, Miss Anthony, and Mrs. Joslyn Gage, there is this fitting tribute to her: "Abby Kelley was the most untiring and most persecuted of all the women who labored throughout the anti-slavery struggle. She traveled up and down alike in winter's cold and summer's heat, with scorn, ridicule, violence and mobs accompanying her, suffering all kinds of persecution, still speaking whenever and wherever she gained an audience—in the open air, in school house, barn, depot, church, or public hall, on week day or Sunday, as she found opportunity." And, incredible as it will soon seem, if it does not appear so already, "for listening to her on Sunday many men and women were expelled from their churches."

When the abolitionists of Rhode Island were seeking to defeat the restricted constitution of the Dorr party,[1] Abby Kelley was more than once mobbed in the old town hall in the city of Providence, and pelted with bad eggs.

And what can be said of the gifted authoress of "Uncle Tom's Cabin," Harriet Beecher Stowe?[2] Happy woman must she be that to her was given the power in such unstinted measure to touch and move the popular heart! More than to reason or religion are we indebted to the influence which this wonderful delineation of American chattel slavery produced on the public mind.

Nor must I omit to name the daughter of the excellent Myron Holley, who in her youth and beauty espoused the cause of the slave,[3] nor of Lucy Stone and Antoinette Brown, for when the slave had few friends and advocates they were noble enough to speak their best word in his behalf.

Others there were who, though they were not known on the platform, were none the less earnest and effective for anti-slavery in their more retired lives. There were many such to greet me and welcome me to my newly-found heritage of freedom. They met me as a brother, and by their kind consideration did much to make endurable the rebuffs I encountered elsewhere. At the anti-slavery office in Providence, Rhode Island, I remember with a peculiar interest Lucinda Wilmarth, whose acceptance of life's duties and labors, and whose heroic struggle with sickness and death, taught me more than one lesson; and Amorancy Paine, never weary in performing any service, however arduous, which fidelity to the slave demanded of her. Then there were Phebe Jackson, Elizabeth Chace, the Sisson sisters, the Chases, the Greenes, the Browns, the Goolds, the Shoves, the Anthonys, the Roses, the Fayerweathers, the Motts, the Earles, the Spooners, the Southwicks, the Buffums, the Fords, the Wilburs, the Henshaws, the Burgesses, and others whose names are lost, but whose deeds are living yet in the regenerated life of our new republic cleansed from the curse and sin of slavery.

*Life and Times of Frederick Douglass*, pp. 579-584

# HARRIET TUBMAN[4]

Rochester, August 29, 1868.

Dear Harriet:

I am glad to know that the story of your eventful life has been written by a kind lady, and that the same is soon to be published. You ask for what you do not need when you call upon me for a word of commendation. I need such words from you far more than you can need them from me, especially where your superior labors and devotion to the cause of the lately enslaved of our land are known as I know them. The difference between us is very marked. Most that I have done and suffered in the service of our cause has been in public, and I have received much encouragement at every step of the way. You on the other hand have labored in a private way. I have wrought in the day—you in the night. I have had the applause of the crowd and the satisfaction that comes of being approved by the multitude, while the most that you have done has been witnessed by a few trembling, scarred, and foot-sore bondmen and women, whom you have led out of the house of bondage, and whose heart-felt "God bless you" has been your only reward. The midnight sky and the silent stars have been the witnesses of your devotion to freedom and of your heroism. Excepting John Brown—of sacred memory —I know of no one who has willingly encountered more perils and hardships to serve our enslaved people than you have. Much that you have done would seem improbable to those who do not know you as I know you. It is to me a great pleasure and a great privilege to bear testimony to your character and your works, and to say to those to whom you may come, that I regard you in every way truthful and trustworthy.

Your friend,
Frederick Douglass.

Sarah H. Bradford, *Scenes in the Life of Harriet Tubman* (Auburn, N.Y., 1869), pp. 7-8

MYRTILLA MINER[5]

Washington, D.C., May 4, 1883.

Dear Friend:[6]

You have often urged me to tell you the little (and it is but little) I remember of Miss Myrtilla Miner, the founder of what is now the Normal School for Colored Girls in the city of Washington, D.C. The task is in every sense an agreeable one and should have been performed long ago. The press of more immediate duties or perhaps, to speak more truly, an infirmity of which I am not entirely free, of postponing till tomorrow what ought to be done today is the explanation of my tardy compliance with your request. Your patience, perserverance and continuing prompting have at last set me to work. If we owe it to the generations that go before us, and to those which come after us, to make some record of the good deeds we have met within our journey through life, and perpetuate the memory and example of those who have in a signal manner made themselves serviceable to suffering humanity, we certainly should not forget the brave little woman, who first invaded the city of Washington to establish here a school for the education of a class long despised and neglected. As I look back, to the moral surroundings of the time when that school was begun, the state of public sentiment in the North as well as in the South which then existed, how low was the estimation in which colored people were then held, how little sympathy there was with any effort to dispel their ignorance, diminish their hardships, alleviate their suffering and soften their misfortunes, I marvel all the more at the thought, the zeal, the faith and the courage of Myrtilla Miner, in daring to be the pioneer of such a movement for education here in the District of Columbia, the very citadel of slavery, the place most watched and guarded by the slave power and where humane tendencies were more speedily detected and sternly opposed.

It is now more than thirty years (but such have been the changes wrought that it seems a century) since Miss Miner, in company with Joseph and Phoebe Hathaway (brother and sister) called upon me at my printing office in Rochester, New York and found me at work busily mailing my paper *The North Star*. It was my custom to continue my work no matter who came and hence I barely looked up to give them welcome, supposing the call to be an ordinary one, perhaps of sympathy with my work, or more likely an act of mere curiosity. So I went on with my work. I was not long however permitted to treat my callers in this unceremonious way. I soon found I was in a presence that demanded my whole attention. A slender, wiry, pale (not over healthy) but singularly animated figure was before me, and startled me with the announcement that she was then on her way to the city of Washington to establish a school for the Education of colored girls. I stopt mailing my paper at once, and gave my attention to what was said. I was amazed and looked to see if the lady was in earnest and meant what she said. The doubt on my mind was transient. I saw at a glance that the fire of enthusiasm lighted in her eye and that the true martyr spirit flamed in her soul. My feelings were those of mingled joy and sadness. Here I thought is another enterprise—wild, dangerous, desperate and impracticable, and destined only to bring failure and suffering. Yet I was deeply moved with admiration by the heroic purpose of the delicate and fragile person who stood or rather moved to and fro before me, for she would not accept a chair. She seemed too full of her enterprise to think of her own ease and hence kept me in motion all the time she was in my office. Mr. and Mrs. Hathaway remained silent, Miss Miner and myself did the talking. She advocated the feasibility of her enterprise and I (timid and faithless) opposed it in all earnestness. She said she knew the South. She had lived among Slaveholders. She had even taught slaves to read in Mississippi and she was not afraid of violence in the District of Columbia. To me the proposition was reckless almost to the point of madness. In my fancy I saw this Slaveholding malice and possibly beaten down by the mob. The fate of Prudence Crandall in Connecticut[7] and the then recent case of Mrs. Douglass at Norfolk[8] was before me, and my own experience in attempting to teach a Sunday School in St. Michaels[9] came before me. Her resolution was taken and was not to be changed nor shaken, and the result I need not say has justified her determination. I give you this leaf for your book if you ever carry out your purpose to write some account of the life and works of this rare and remarkable woman.

I never pass the Miner Normal School for colored girls in this city without a feeling of self reproach that I could have said ought to quench the zeal, shake the faith, and quail the courage of the Noble woman by whom it was founded and whose name it bears.

Truly yours,
Frederick Douglass

*Ms.*, Frederick Douglass Papers, Library of Congress,
Manuscripts Division, Washington, D.C.

## IDA B. WELLS[10]

Cedar Hill, Anacostia, D.C., Oct. 25, 1892

Dear Miss Wells:

Let me give you thanks for your faithful paper on the lynch abomination now generally practiced against colored people in the South. There has been no word equal to it in convincing power. I have spoken, but my word is feeble in comparison. You give us what you know and testify from actual knowledge. You have dealt with the facts with cool, painstaking fidelity and left those naked and uncontradicted facts to speak for themselves.

Brave woman! You have done your people and mine a service which can neither be weighed nor measured. If American conscience were only half alive, if the American church and clergy were only half christianized, if American moral responsibility were not hardened by persistent infliction of outrage and crime against colored people, a scream of horror, shame and indignation would rise to Heaven wherever your pamphlet shall be read.

But alas! even crime has power to reproduce itself and create conditions favorable to its own existence. It sometimes seems we are deserted by earth and Heaven—yet we must still think, speak and work, and trust in the power of a merciful God for final deliverance.

Very truly and gratefully yours,
Frederick Douglass

*Ms.*, Moorland Collection, Howard University Library;
printed in Ida B. Wells, *Southern Horrors.*
*Lynch Law in All Its Phases* (New York, 1892), p. 4

# ELIZABETH CADY STANTON

Washington, D.C., October 22, 1885

To the Editor of the New Era,

I make haste to ask an inch or two of your precious space, to join with her many friends in tendering sincere congratulations to Mrs. Elizabeth Cady Stanton on her 70th anniversary, and give her joy that she still lives, and that she is likely to tarry within the gates of life, long enough to see the fulfilment of her hopes and labors for the complete Emancipation and enfranchisement of woman. I am no stranger to the life and work of that excellent lady, and am proud to be one of the great cloud of witnesses who will on her 70th birthday, bear ample testimony to her high character as a woman, and to her immeasurable services to the cause of woman, as an advocate. Five and forty years ago in Boston, before the snows of time had settled upon the locks of either of us and before the cause of woman had taken its place among the reforms of the nineteenth century, Mrs. Stanton, then just returned from her wedding tour in Europe, sat by my side and taught me the new Gospel of woman's rights. I was then only a few years out Slavery, and I freshly remembered the lash and sting of bondage at the South, and the intense bitterness of the popular prejudice against color at the North, and was all the more ready to listen to, and learn of such a beautiful teacher. Perhaps, no man is more a debtor to Mrs. Stanton for her noble work in the world, than myself. While she clothed woman in my mind with a dignity and grandeur which I had not before recognized, she gave me a higher conception of my own worth by disregarding popular prejudice and taking pains to impart to me the great truths with which her mind was illuminated. It is sometimes said that women do not appreciate greatness in individuals of their own sex. I hope their utterances on the 70th anniversary of Elizabeth Cady Stanton will silence the slanders. Honor to whom honor.

Respectfully yours,
Fredk Douglass

Ms., Frederick Douglass Papers, Library of
Congress, Manuscripts Division, Washington, D.C.

## THE MERITS OF LUCY STONE
Speech delivered at National-American Memorial Service
at Washington, D.C., March, 1894

We do well to cherish and preserve the memory of good men and
women who have filled up the measure of their years with effective
service to mankind and have passed away. In doing this we discharge
a duty to the living not less sacred than that we owe to the noble
dead. We are all the better to-day for devoting this hour to the
memory of the cause of liberty and of woman suffrage. We are not
yet so abundant in such workers as not to miss the presence and feel
the loss of those who have performed signal service in our cause.

Especially is it fitting that we pause for the moment and recall to
memory one so distinguished for service as she who was so lately
with us and who has been so recently and so suddenly called away.
We can not soon forget the voice, the face and form of the remarkable personage to whom we so long looked, and never in vain, for
wise counsel and noble inspiration in work for advancement of
woman.

There has been no time during the last thirty years that the name
of Lucy Stone has not been a tower of strength to the woman suffrage movement. Though she had reached and passed her three-
score and ten, her departure from us was felt as a surprise as well as
a loss. When I saw her at Chicago last summer she looked the picture
of health, and gave promise of much valuable service to the cause
of woman. We have some consolation in the fact that she lived to
see the dawn of the triumph of the cause she had so much at heart.
We may also console ourselves by the thought that she did her
work so well in life that she has left behind her thousands upon
thousands of converts to take up that work and carry it to success.
In New England especially, the scene of her labors, she has left a
great crowd of witnesses to the truth she served so faithfully, and
which she endeavored so wisely to organize into law for the better
government of mankind.

I can add but little to what has already been said of the merits of
Lucy Stone. Her memory is safe in the hands of those who have
spoken and who shall speak. They have stood nearer to her great
life work than I have, and knew her much better than I did. I knew
her better in her earlier public career and in her anti-slavery efforts

than in her later life as a lecturer, organizer and editor. In this last field of service I have seen her mainly from a distance, and have had only a partial view of her devotion and efficiency in that peculiar work, the work with which her name and memory will be chiefly and forever associated. Her services are known and read of all men. They have won for her a name and fame which time cannot dim and which history will not allow to die. To appreciate the noble character of Lucy Stone some account must be taken of the peculiar circumstances in which she espoused the great cause for which she mainly employed her voice and pen. It was not very popular at that time to advocate the right of suffrage for woman.

But Lucy Stone was not a woman of one idea alone. She comprehended the claims of human liberty and human brotherhood on all their many sides. She acknowledged manhood under whatever color or race it might come. Her first work was for the anti-slavery cause. Here she gained her first distinction as a public speaker. Were she here with us to-day, she would resent with proper spirit the indignity offered at the Riggs House the other day to a colored lady, an honored member of this Association.

Lucy Stone came into the anti-slavery movement just at a time when her presence and her work were most needed. It was an hour of moral darkness and doubt. It was when slavery was in the prime of its power; when the most extraordinary efforts were being made to put down the anti-slavery agitation, and to suppress the anti-slavery sentiment of the country; when the Whig party and the Democratic party had announced in their platforms their purpose to accomplish this suppression at all hazards; when the inhuman fugitive slave bill was in full force; when leading divines and statesmen were endeavoring to reconcile the people of the North to that infamous measure; when slave hunters were abroad in the land endeavoring to recapture and return slaves to their masters, and when it seemed that the cause of the slave must perish or be postponed to future generations, it was then that Lucy Stone, with all the freshness of her youth, maidenly grace, and heroic courage, stepped to the very front of our anti-slavery platform and became one of our most attractive and effective advocates. Her advent, like that of Mrs. Stowe's great book, *Uncle Tom's Cabin*, jointed well with the extreme needs of the times. No one ever came into that movement who at once arrested a more widespread attention than did Lucy Stone. Calls came for her from all parts of the Northern States. She was everywhere in request. Everybody wanted to hear this new voice on the anti-slavery question. Her responses to these calls were most generous and successful. She was greeted everywhere by crowded houses. It was hers to work in season and out of season, and she did it nobly and without grudging. I certainly deemed her advent among us a great accession to our anti-slavery forces, and was much encouraged by her glorious presence in the work of emancipation. She not only instantly and broadly arrested public attention to the anti-slavery question, but she retained for herself a firm hold up on the public mind as long as she devoted her eloquence to this reform.

Of her work in the cause of woman I leave others to speak more fully than I can. While I sincerely admire her work for woman suffrage, you will pardon me if my tribute to her is mainly due for what she was and what she did for the cause of the slave in the dark hours of his need. It was Lucy Stone's good fortune, while always earnest and uncompromising either in the cause of woman or the cause of the slave, never to create for herself any avoidable opposition, either by intemperance of speech, personal peculiarities, or by the manner of her public addresses. She had decided advantage both in voice and in person. To listen to her at that time was like listening to delightful music. Her temper was even and her spirit persuasive. She was not of those who measure their progress by the resistance they meet in contending for the cause, though at times it is an invaluable rule. My first acquaintance with her began more than forty years ago when she and the late Miss Sally Holley were acquiring a college education at Oberlin, O.[11] At that early day I found her endowed with the idea of equal rights for woman, and what at that time pleased me most I confess was this, I found her a radical abolitionist. From that day I have never lost sight of Lucy Stone. Her figure in one or the other of those great movements has been permanently in my mind. Few if any have done better work for either cause than has Lucy Stone. As one of the millions, therefore, for whose freedom she nobly battled and for whom she stood with a zeal as warm and a soul as strong as any of the brave men and women of our anti-slavery phalanx, I am glad to be allowed an humble part in these memorial services which are now and hereafter to form an interesting and impressive chapter in the history of the woman suffrage movement in America.

It is not alone on the goodness of any cause that men can safely predicate success. Much depends upon the character and quality of the men and women who are its advocates. The Redeemer must ever come from above. Only the best of mankind can afford to support unpopular opinions. The common sort will drift with the time. No good cause can fail when supported by such women as were Lucretia Mott, Abby Kelley, Angelina Grimké, Lydia Maria Child, Maria W. Chapman, Thankful Southwick, Sally Holley, Ernestine L. Rose,[12] E. Oakes Smith, Elizabeth P. Peabody, and the noble and gifted Lucy Stone. Not only have we a glorious constellation of women on the silent continent to assure us that our cause is good, and that it must finally prevail, but we have such men as William Lloyd Garrison, Wendell Phillips, William Henry Channing, Francis Jackson, Gerrit Smith, Samuel J. May, and Samuel E. Sewall, now no longer with us in body, but in spirit and memory, to cheer us on in the good work of lifting women in the fullest sense to the dignity of American liberty and American citizenship.

*The Woman's Journal.*[13] March 24, 1894

## NOTES

1. At first, the abolitionists participated actively in the struggle led by Thomas Wilson Dorr in 1841 for a wider extension of the limited franchise in Rhode Island. But when the "People's party" denied the suffrage to blacks in the new constitution which the Dorrites submitted to the vote of the people, the anti-slavery forces felt betrayed and called for defeat of the constitution. Douglass and Abby Kelley were active in the campaign and toured Rhode Island against the constitution.

2. Harriet Beecher Stowe (1811-1896), daughter of Lyman Beecher and sister of Henry Ward Beecher, became an ardent abolitionist and world-famous as the author of *Uncle Tom's Cabin.* Although her book sold hundreds of thousands of copies, Mrs. Stowe never benefited financially.

3. The reference is to Sally Holley.

4. Harriet Tubman (c. 1821-1913) was the legendary "conductor" on the Underground Railroad. She was born a slave on the eastern shore of Maryland, fled from slavery when nearly thirty years of age, and devoted herself to guiding others to freedom. Known as the "Moses" of her people, she made nineteen journeys into slave territory during a period of ten years and brought back more than three hundred men, women, and children. During the Civil War she served as a military scout and nurse to the Union armies.

Douglass also sent a brief letter to Sojourner Truth (c. 1797-1883) to be used in her *Narrative of Sojourner Truth*. Born a slave in New York, she was freed when the state liberated its slaves in 1827. She became an active abolitionist and woman's rights advocate, changing her slave name from Isabella to Sojourner Truth. In his letter, Douglass praised her for being "as usual, full of noble purposes, looking to the welfare of suffering men and women" (*Narrative of Sojourner* [Battle Creek, Michigan, 1884], p. 265).

5. Myrtilla Miner (1815-1864), born in Brookfield, New York, was profoundly influenced by her contact with Negro slavery when she was teaching at a school in Whitesville, Mississippi. She began a campaign for Negro education, but returned North after learning that teaching a slave to read was a criminal offense in Mississippi. Though very ill, she was determined to start a normal school for colored girls in Washington, D.C., a stronghold of aristocratic, pro-slavery feelings. On December 3, 1851, in a small apartment, she opened her normal school for free black girls. In spite of constant attacks, the school grew and in 1871 was joined with Howard University. In 1879, as the Miner Normal School (now Miner Teachers' College), it became part of the public school system of the District of Columbia.

6. Mrs. Ellen M. O'Connor was the author of *Myrtilla Miner: A Memoir*, published in 1885.

7. In 1831, Prudence Crandall (1803-1889) opened a school for girls in Canterbury, Connecticut. She allowed a black girl to attend, and then, when protests arose, decided to keep a school for Negroes only. The town opposed her, but she persisted. A law was passed by the state legislature on May 24, 1833, which made it illegal for anyone to set up a school for colored people who were not inhabitants of the state without the consent of the selectmen of the town in which the school was to be located. Under this law, she was arrested and imprisoned, and the lower court of Connecticut ruled against her. In July 1834, the Supreme Court of Connecticut reversed the decision of the lower court on the grounds of insufficient evidence, but did not rule on the constitutionality of the law itself. Crandall was finally forced to abandon her school.

8. Mrs. Margaret Douglass and her daughter had conducted a school in Norfolk for Negro children. In 1853, she was indicted by a grand jury for violating the Virginia laws. She determined not to hire a lawyer but to plead her own case. So effective was her argument in her behalf that the jury recommended a nominal punishment, but the judge imposed a sentence of imprisonment in the city jail for one month. He justified the Virginia law prohibiting Negro education as a necessary measure against northern incendiaries bent upon abolishing slavery.

9. While a slave, Douglass set up a Sunday School. He had twenty students, but the school lasted only a week. The second Sunday a mob,

headed by Douglass's master and two Methodist class-leaders, invaded the school and drove the students away with stones. They were forbidden ever to meet again. Douglass was accused of emulating Nat Turner, the slave rebel, and was threatened that, like Turner, he too would end on the gallows if he did not take heed.

10. Ida B. Wells (1869-1931) was born in Holly Springs, Mississippi, and after attending Rust College and entering the teaching profession, she moved to Mississippi. She gave up teaching after six years to become editor and half-owner of *Free Speech*, a journal which exposed the evils of lynching. Forced to leave Memphis in 1892 because of her crusade against lynching (her life was threatened), Wells went to New York, where she began lecturing against lynching and published her first pamphlet, *Southern Horrors*, in that same year. After two tours of England to publicize the evils of lynching, in which she was supported by Frederick Douglass, she settled in Chicago in 1895 and married the distinguished black lawyer, Ferdinand Barnett. She continued her anti-lynching crusade, publishing additional pamphlets and speaking to many groups. She was one of the founders of the National Association for the Advancement of Colored People.

11. Oberlin College, a strong anti-slavery and coeducational institution in Ohio, graduated many of the foremost abolitionists and woman's rights leaders. Oberlin was a center of abolitionism and a station on the Underground Railroad.

12. Ernestine Louise Potowski Rose (1810-1892) was a pioneer of woman's rights, an early advocate of the free public school system, and a staunch supporter of the abolitionists. Born in a Polish ghetto, where her father was a rabbi, she left home and settled in England where she came under the influence of Robert Owen, the Utopian Socialist and leader of the British reform movement. She married in England and with her husband came to the United States where she spent the rest of her life except for a short visit abroad. In this country, she became active in all of the reform movements of her time.

13. With her husband, Lucy Stone was editor of *The Woman's Journal*.

# APPENDIX: TWO BLACK WOMEN DISCUSS FREDERICK DOUGLASS AS A CHAMPION OF THE WOMAN SUFFRAGE MOVEMENT

## MRS. ROSA H. HAZEL AT DOUGLASS MEMORIAL MEETING, ST. PAUL, MINNESOTA

The following paper was recently read by Mrs. Rosa H. Hazel, at a Douglass Memorial meeting, held under the auspices of the A.L.E. League of Minnesota,[1] and owing to the very able and interesting manner in which she discusses the great liberator in relation to the woman suffrage question, we are pleased to publish the paper for the paper for the benefit of our readers, especially those who are interested in Woman Suffrage.

Mrs. Hazel, whose cut we present herewith, is an enthusiastic advocate of Woman's Rights and is ever ready to support any movement that is fostered to emancipate those of her sex; she is an indefatigable worker in the interest of her race and can justly be characterized a race woman, for she has demonstrated that she is in full sympathy with every cause appertaining to the elevation of the race; she is a woman of education, culture and refinement, and of great individuality. Such women as Mrs. Hazel would reflect credit upon any race, and it is with a deep sense of pride in her inestimable value to the race that we bear such testimony to her excellent qualities.

—Editor, *Twin City American*[2]

Mr. President, Ladies and Gentlemen: I am requested to give a brief account of Frederick Douglass in his relation to the woman movement.

In the anti-slavery movement of fifty years ago arose a schism. Strange as it may seem to us, who are used to the larger latitude accorded woman, the freer scope in which to rise to the possibilities within her, in those dark days of the nation, when the South, with fierce persistency, and the North, with servile acquiescence, were forging the chain of the slave, invoking gods, both Greek and Christian, to testify to his inherent inferiority, the anti-slavery workers were suddenly awakened to a new danger menacing them.

In an organization dedicated to the cause of the slave,—a cause appealing in its romantic, yet tragic, history, to all within us that was holy, tender, merciful,—it were, indeed, strange if woman found no place for labor and for sacrifice. And so we find her attending the anti-slavery meetings; listening with bated breath to the thrilling stories of escaped slaves; the fiery denunciations of Garrison; the fiercely just invective of Phillips; the scholarly argument of Theodore D. Weld;[3] the passionate plea of Angelina Grimpke [sic] and others whose names are now revered household words. We find her leaving homes of luxury, literary careers, scenes of social triumphs, to give time, thought, money, influence, even life if necessary, to the blotting out of a nation's sin, the purifying of a nation's life.

But the time inevitably came when the women working in the anti-slavery cause were impelled by the logic of events to seek a voice in the general body of anti-slavery workers, in order to make their work more efficient and harmonious. At that time there were some earnest, sincere men who felt that the dividing line of sex privileges should be drawn, when woman sought recognition as an equal factor, even in this movement for human liberty. So the little cloud, no larger than a man's hand, grew and overshadowed the cause, crippling at one time its unity and efficiency.

The woman who would battle for the freedom of the slave soon found that, woven in that seamless robe of liberty, was another golden thread, and that she herself worked with fettered limbs, and unworthily, until her own individuality was recognized, her own freedom accomplished. So the long struggle began which has opened up so many opportunities for women and is still working out its own and the nation's salvation—the at-one-ment of humanity, the perfect whole in the body politic, the ideal government of a free people.

The division in the ranks of the American Anti-Slavery Society in 1840 was followed by a more pronounced hostility to the equal representation of women in the World's Anti-Slavery Convention, held in London the same year, at which, after a bitter discussion, the women delegates from America were rejected.

Men, who afterwards so nobly championed woman's cause, were at this time in all stages of development on the vexed question, from utter hostility to a conservative estimate of woman's needs and rights. So, only two of the American delegates, Wm. Lloyd Garrison and Nathaniel P. Rogers, refused to take part in the convention, remaining with the ostracized women, silent spectators in a meeting, the subject of which lay so near their hearts.[4]

It was then that Lucretia Mott and Elizabeth Cady Stanton resolved to hold a woman's rights convention on their return to America, and in 1848 the first woman's rights convention was held in Seneca Falls, N.Y. Among the speakers at this now historic meeting was Frederick Douglass. In the declarations and resolutions adopted at this convention the demand was made for "equal rights in the universities, trades, professions; in the suffrage; in political offices, honors and emoluments; complete equality in marriage, personal freedom, property, wages, children, to make contracts, to sue and be sued, and to testify in courts of justice."

In the advocacy of these resolutions, Frederick Douglass was earnest and convincing. Side by side with Lucretia Mott and Elizabeth Cady Stanton, he worked for their adoption. In an editorial in his paper, *The North Star,* he says: "Many who have at last discovered that the negroes have some rights as well as other members of the human family, have yet to be convinced that women are entitled to any." Eight years ago, a number of persons of this description actually abandoned the A[nti] S[lavery] cause, lest by giving their influence in that direction, they might possibly be giving countenance to the dangerous heresy that woman, in respect to rights, should be equal to man.

In the chemistry of his own soul did he find the affinity between the rights of the negro and the rights of woman. He, himself, was ready; the "woman question," as it was called, was only the opportunity for a broader declaration of the doctrine of human rights. The protest began against chattel slavery could not end there, but must ever be a protest against all slavery, whether of race, sex or opinions. When I hear women, in indignant amazement, censure the apathy of their own sex on this vital question, and the indifference of negro men to one of the gravest problems of the day, I answer, "The negro is not unrepresented in your fight for freedom." Not alone did Douglass, a slave, but Sojourner Truth, also a slave, with Purvis,[5] Remond, and other free-born colored men and women, have borne witness for woman and labored for her enfranchisement.

And I aver that a subject class is always a servile class. It accepts prevailing standards; it creates none of its own. The restless ones that will not stay in it are looked upon with askance, and it takes long years of fiery trial for the leaven of noble discontent to work its way through the mass.

### A Subject Class Always Degrades Its Own.

Woman's long subjectivity has benumbed her. That so many have passed without the border, are making progress all along the line, is the beginning of the end of her long subjection. The slave, the freedman, among the negroes, has, to my mind, less excuse for an attitude of indifference to the political inferiority of woman, in that his own escape from bondage has been largely due to her efforts; his own enfranchisement has been to him the precious sign of his manhood, the coveted goal of his ambition. He, in his own person, knows the degradation of disfranchisement, the futility of uncitizenship in a country where the ballot is the peaceful weapon in the adjustment of his grievances, the preservation of his rights.

"Ingrate would I be," said Douglass, "if I failed in my duty to fight for these women in my hour of triumph, who, when the shackles were on my limbs, fought for me and mine."

### Woman's Duty

The negro woman should stand shoulder to shoulder with the negro man in the struggle for race development and race recognition. Let the Caucasian, if he will, refuse justice to his women; but never let it be said that the negro, from the height of his suddenly gotten vantage ground—in the dazzling light of his new possession—forget the mother who bore him, the wife who shares his burdens; the sister and daughter, who, with longing eyes, turn to the horizon and wait and work for the dawning of a juster, freer day.

Let me commend to you the words of Douglass, when he said: "I believed that the exclusion of my race from participation in government was not only a wrong but a great mistake, because it took from that race motives for high thought and endeavor and degraded them in the eyes of the world around them. If from the cradle through life the outside world brands a class as unfit for this or that work, the character of the class will come to resemble and conform to the character described. I would give woman a vote precisely as I insisted upon giving the colored man the right to vote, in order that she shall have the same motives for making herself a useful citizen as those in force in the case of other citizens. In this denial of the right to participate in government, not merely the degradation of woman and the perpetuation of a great injustice happens, but the maiming and repudiation of one-half of the moral and intellectual power of the government of the world. Thus far all human governments have been failures, for none have secured, except in a partial degree, the ends for which governments are instituted."

### Standard by Which Douglass' Greatness Shall be Determined.

When the final verdict shall have been passed on Douglass and his work, it may be that future biographers may think that the greatness of Douglass lay not alone in a life-long consecration for the elevation of his race, but in the breadth of view of this man of the people, who reached out not only for the good of the negro race, but had the wisdom to foresee the larger good to be accomplished in that kind of justice which ignores both race and sex, giving to all equal opportunities, obligations and incentives in this country.

Rosa Hazard Hazel.

*Twin City American*, Minneapolis and St. Paul, May 4, 1899

## FREDERICK DOUGLASS

### by Mary Church Terrell

Mary Church Terrell was born in Memphis at the end of the Civil War. Her mother had been educated in slavery and her father, Robert R. Church, Sr., was the son of a pro-Union slaveowner, who made a fortune in real estate. Mary was sent to the North for schooling at six. After being graduated from Oberlin College, she taught at Wilberforce University and at a colored high school in Washington, D.C. She married Robert J. Terrell, a black graduate of Harvard University, who became a municipal judge in Washington, a position he occupied for twenty years. Active in work among Negro women, Mrs. Terrell was elected the first president of the National Association of Colored Women in which position she actively fought Jim-Crow and joined forces with white women in the Woman Suffrage cause. In 1908, at the celebration marking the sixtieth anniversary of the first Woman's Rights Convention at Seneca Falls, New York, Mrs. Terrell delivered an address lauding the role of Frederick Douglass in the struggle for the right of women to vote.

There are two reasons why I look back upon the meeting of which this is the sixtieth anniversary with genuine pleasure and glowing pride. In the first place, I am a woman like Elizabeth Cady Stanton. In the second place, I belong to the race of which Frederick Douglass was such a magnificent representative. Perhaps I should be too modest to proclaim from the housetops that I think I have a decided advantage over everybody else who participates in this anniversary to-day. Perhaps I should be too courteous and generous to call attention to the fact that I have one more reason for being proud of that record-breaking history making meeting, which was held in this city 60 years ago, than anybody else who takes part in these exercises to-day. But I simply cannot resist the temptation to show that this is one occasion on which a colored woman really has good and sufficient reasons for feeling several inches taller than her sisters of the more favored race. It so rarely happens that a colored women in the United States can prove by convincing, indisputable facts that she has good reasons for being proud of the race with which she is identified that you will pardon me for the pride I feel on this occasion, I am sure.

The incomparable Frederick Douglass did many things of which I as a member of that race which he served so faithfully and well am proud. But there is nothing he ever did in his long and brilliant career in which I take keener pleasure and greater pride than I do in his ardent advocacy of equal political rights for women and the effective service he rendered the cause of woman suffrage sixty years ago. Even though some of us have passed that period in our lives, when we take much pleasure in those old romances which describe in such deliciously thrilling details those days of old, when knights were bold and had a chronic habit of rescuing fair ladies in high towers in distress, still I am sure there is nobody here to-day with soul so dead and heart so cold who does not admire a man who, in the everyday affairs of this prosaic world, rushes gallantly to the assistance of a woman fighting to the death for a principal as dear to her as life and actually succeeds in helping her establish and maintain it, in spite of the opposition of even her faithful coadjutors and her most faithful friends. This is precisely the service which Frederick Douglass rendered Elizabeth Cady Stanton at that Seneca Falls meeting sixty years ago.

When the defeat of that resolution which demanded equal political rights for women seemed imminent, because some of the most ardent advocates of woman suffrage deemed it untimely and unwise, when even dear, broad, brave Lucretia Mott tried to dissuade Mrs. Stanton, to whom it was the very heart and soul of the movement, from insisting upon it by declaring "Lizzie, thee will make us all ridiculous," I am glad that it was to a large extent due to Frederick Douglass' masterful arguments and matchless eloquence that it was carried, in spite of the opposition of its equally conscientious and worthy foes. And I am as proud of Elizabeth Cady Stanton, as a woman, as I am of Frederick Douglass, the Negro. Try as hard as we may, it is difficult for women of the present day to imagine what courage and strength of mind it required for Elizabeth Cady Stanton to demand equal political rights for her sex at that time.

It is safe to assert that there is not a single woman here to-day who would not have uttered the same words of warning and caution as did Lucretia Mott if she had been present, when a sister made demands which seemed so utterly impossible and rashly extravagant as were those urged by Elizabeth Cady Stanton at a meeting in which for the first time in the history of the world it was openly, boldly proclaimed without any qualifications and reservations whatsoever, that women on general principles had as much right to choose the rulers and make laws as had men, and that it was the duty of American women in particular to do everything in their power to secure the elective franchise for themselves. And this little episode with which we are all so familiar should not cause us to love those who opposed the resolution demanding equal political rights for women the less but should cause us to praise and admire those who insisted upon its adoption, the more.

It is difficult for us to exaggerate the importance of the bold step taken by the advocates of this resolution, when they dared to array themselves against their friends who they knew were as interested in woman suffrage as themselves and as willing to make sacrifices to effect it as were they themselves. And for that reason there are no words of praise too strong to bestow on that great woman and that illustrious man who finally succeeded in convincing their friends in that meeting that the course they advised was the wisest and the best. How glad we all are to-day that Martha C. Wright, Mary Ann Mc-Clintock, Lucretia Mott and Elizabeth Cady Stanton dared to offend the tender, delicate sensibilities and shock the proprieties of this staid, inconsistently proper and hypocritical old world.

But if Elizabeth Cady Stanton manifested sublime courage and au-dacious contempt for the ridicule and denunciation she knew would be heaped upon her as a woman, how much more were such qualities displayed by Frederick Douglass, the ex-slave. It is doubtful if Fred-erick Douglass' independence of spirit and sense of justice were ever put to a severer test than they were on that day, when for the first time in his life, he publicly committed himself to the cause of woman suffrage. I have always extracted great pleasure from the thought not only that Frederick Douglass, and he alone of all men present at the Seneca Falls meeting, was conspicuous for his enthusiastic advocacy of equal political rights for women, but that he found it in his heart to advocate it ever afterward with such ardor and zeal.

In no half-hearted way did he lay hold of the newly-proclaimed doctrine, nor did he ever try to conceal his views. When nearly all the newspapers, big and little, good, bad and indifferent were hurling jibes and jeers at the women and the men who participated in the Seneca Falls meeting, there was one newspaper, which was published in Rochester, N. Y., which not only heartily commended the leaders, in the new movement but warmly espoused their cause. This was Frederick Douglass' *North Star*. In the leading editorial July 28, 1848, after declaring, "we could not do justice to our own convictions nor to the excellent persons connected with the infant movement, if we did not in this connection offer a few remarks on the general subject which the convention met to consider and the objects it seeks to attain." As editor of the *North Star*, Mr. Douglass expresses his views as follows: "A discussion of the rights of animals would be regarded with far more complacency by many of what are called the wise and good of the land than would be a discussion of the rights of women. Many who have at last made the discovery that Negroes have some rights as well as other members of the human family have yet to be convinced that women have any. Standing as we do upon the watch tower of human freedom, we cannot be deterred from an expression of our approbation of any movement, however humble, to improve and elevate any member of the human family."

In his autobiography which was published in 1882 Mr. Douglass thus explains how he first became interested in the cause of woman suffrage "Observing woman's agency, devotion and efficiency in pleading the cause of the slave, gratitude for this high service early moved me to give favorable attention to the subject of what is called 'Woman's Rights' and caused me to be denominated a woman's rights man." "I am glad to say," he adds, "that I have never been ashamed to be thus designated." To Mrs. Elizabeth Cady Stanton Mr. Douglass always attributed his first conversion to the cause of woman suffrage. And so eager was he that Mrs. Stanton should know that he had referred to this in his book that he wrote her a letter February 6, 1882, calling her attention to that fact. "You will observe," he said "that I don't forget my walk with you from the house of Mr. Joseph Southwick, where you quietly brought to my notice your arguments for womanhood suffrage. That is forty years ago. You had just returned from your European tour. From that conversation with you I have been convinced of the wisdom of woman suffrage and I have never denied the faith."

If at any time Mr. Douglass seemed to waver in his allegiance to the cause of political enfranchisement of women, it was because he realized as no white person, no matter how broad and sympathetic he may be, has ever been able to feel or can possibly feel today just what it means to belong to my despised, handicapped and persecuted race. I am woman and I know what it means to be circumscribed, deprived, handicapped and fettered on account of my sex. But I assure you that no where in the United States have my feelings been so lacerated, my spirit so crushed, my heart so wounded, no where have I been so humiliated and handicapped on account of my sex as I have been on account of my race. I can readily understand, therefore, what feelings must have surged through Frederick Douglass' heart, and I can almost feel the intensity of the following words he uttered, when he tried to explain why he honestly thought it was more necessary and humane to give the ballot to the Negro than to women, for the law makers of this country were too narrow and ungenerous to deal justly both by the oppressed race and the handicapped, disfranchised sex at one and the same time. "I must say," declared Mr. Douglass, "that I cannot see how any one can pretend that there is the same urgency in giving the ballot to woman as to the Negro. With us," he said, "the matter is a question of life and death at best in fifteen states of the union. When women, because they are women, are hunted down through the streets of New York and New Orleans; their children torn from their arms and their brains dashed out on the pavement; when they are objects of insult and outrage at every turn; when they are in danger of having their houses burnt down over their heads; when their children are not allowed to enter school; then they will have an urgency to obtain the ballot equal to our own." "Is that not also true about black women?" somebody in the audience inquired. "Yes, yes, yes," replied Mr. Douglass, "but not because they are women, but because they are black."

Now I am not trying to minimize in the slightest degree the crime against American women, particularly intelligent women, perpetrated by the law-makers of this country, who for years have refused to allow women to exercise the rights and privileges already guaranteed them in the constitution of the United States. For I have placed myself in that glorious company of eminent American jurists who insist that the 14th amendment extends its privileges and benefactions to women as well as to colored men. As a woman I can readily understand the keen disappointment experienced by those women who had worked so indefatigably, so conscientiously and so long to secure equal political rights for their sex. I can understand their bitterness of spirit, too, when the right of citizenship was coldly withheld from them and conferred upon a race just emerging from bondage, the masses of whose men were densely ignorant—could neither read nor write. But I know that along with such staunch and sterling advocates of woman suffrage as was Wendell Phillips, Wm. Lloyd Garrison, Gerrit Smith and others, Mr. Douglass was as firmly and honestly convinced that his position was scrupulous, wise and just as were the opponents of his view. Those who knew Frederick Douglass best know that he was neither a truckler nor a time-server and that he was incapable of a doing a mean, dishonest act. They know also that he was genuinely interested in the cause of woman suffrage.

When the National American Woman Suffrage Association held its meetings in Washington, or when the National Council of Women met here, if Mr. Douglass were well and at his home, Cedar Hill, I should just as much have expected to see the presidents of those organizations absent from all the meetings as to see Frederick Douglass present at none. If no good thing had come into my life after I went to Washington except the privilege of meeting Frederick Douglass, becoming well-acquainted with him, visiting him in his home and being visited by him in turn—in short the privilege of being included in his list of friends—I should consider that this honor alone would have made my residence in the national capital worth while.

It seems but yesterday when I was present at a meeting of the National Council of Women, Feb. 20th, 1895, and heard when the president remarked that she saw Frederick Douglass in the room and would appoint a committee of two to escort him to the stage. I can see the flutter of white handkerchiefs waved by enthusiastic, admiring women, as the towering, majestic form of Frederick Douglass between the committee of two approached the stage of what is now Columbia Theatre, but what was then called Metzerrott Hall. I can see the handsome, kindly, brown face, surmounted by a shock of snow white hair, as with the grace and courtesy of a Chesterfield he bowed his pleased acknowledgement to the royal Chautauqua salute and the other hearty demonstration which the women made. At the close of the meeting, when Mr. Douglass descended from the stage, he motioned me to wait for him, while he stopped to talk with some of his friends—a request with which I cheerfully complied on that occasion, as on all others, when he honored me by proferring it. As we walked from the hall about two o'clock, Mr. Douglass invited me to lunch with him. Alas, that we cannot know on rare occasions what a day will bring forth. If such knowledge were vouchsafed us, how often would we sacrifice our own feelings and comfort to please a well-beloved friend. Having been indisposed for long time, I felt obliged to decline Mr. Douglass' invitation. How often since that memorable day have I regretted that I did not remain in that inspiring, kingly, kindly presence another short hour. With a courtly sweep of a large, light hat which Mr. Douglass happened to wear, he bade me good-bye, saying as he did so that he was sorry I would not come to see him appease his own hunger, if I didn't care for lunch myself. About nine o'clock that night a friend called at my house to tell me that Mr. Douglass had expired at seven o'clock at his residence just as he was telling Mrs. Douglass the cordial reception accorded him by the National Council of Women.

It has always seemed fitting that a large portion of Frderick Douglass' last day on earth should have been spent at a meeting of an organization founded for the purpose of advancing the interests and promoting the welfare of women—a subject in which he had been interested and a cause for which he had worked so enthusiastically for many years.

If Frederick Douglass were here in the flesh to-day, I am sure he would urge us to buckle on the armor and go forth with fresh courage and renewed zeal to throttle the giants of prejudice, proscription and persecution on account of either sex or race. In Mr. Douglass' own fight from the degradation, the blight and the curse of slavery to freedom, he has set us an example of determination, energy, resolution, faith and hope which we should do well to imitate to-day. Catching the spirit of that great and good man, let us resolve here and now that neither principalities nor powers, nor things present, nor things to come shall separate us from our beloved cause and deter us from discharging the obligations and duties to it which rest upon us to-day.

*Centennial Anniversary of Seneca County and Auxiliary Papers,* Seneca Falls Historical Society, Seneca Falls, New York, 1908, pp. 54-58.

## NOTES

1. The A.L.E. League of Minnesota was a Negro civil rights organization.

2. The *Twin City American* was a black weekly published in Minneapolis and St. Paul.

3. Theodore Dwight Weld (1803-1895) was one of the outstanding abolitionists of the 1830s and the organizer of the "Lane Rebels" who seceded from the Lane Theological Seminary in Cincinnati because of its stand on slavery. He also helped found Oberlin College. His fame as a lecturer and as the author of *American Slavery as It Is* (1833) was considerable, but his voice gave out and he abandoned the lecture platform in the 1840s. Weld married Angelina Grimké.

4. This is not accurate. Charles Lenox Remond also refused to take his seat because the women were excluded.

5. Robert Purvis (1810-1898) was the son of a white South Carolina merchant and a Moorish-Jewish woman whose mother had been a slave. Independently wealthy and so light-skinned that he could have passed for white, he devoted himself to fighting against slavery and discrimination against free blacks. He was the head of the Pennsylvania branch of the Underground Railroad, a founder of the American Anti-Slavery Society, and a supporter of William Lloyd Garrison. Purvis also spoke in favor of woman's rights.

# INDEX

economic discrimination against black women, 107-09; considered foremost male champion of women's rights, ix; continues to be active in woman's rights movement after split with Garrison, 23-24; criticizes exclusion of men by women in temperance society, 60-63; criticizes Lucy Stone, 19, 67-73, 74-77; criticizes woman's rights leaders, 18-19; death, 40-41, 180-81; defended in split with feminists, 79-80; defends woman's right to vote, 130-47; demands woman suffrage, 95-98; describes his first wife, 21-22; early life in slavery, 8-9; on economic discrimination against women, 107-09; escapes from slavery, 9; explains why he supports woman's rights, 105-07; favors "absolute justice and perfect equality for women," x; fears linking Negro and woman suffrage, 131-32; freedom from slavery purchased, 10, 44; furious over Garrison's attack on his domestic life, 20-21; helped by British women, 10; house burned, 38, 47; indebted to women for freedom, 10; in England, 10; learns relationship between discrimination against blacks and discrimination against women, 12; learns to read and write, 9; life as a slave, 168-69; marriage, 9; nominated for vice-president of the United States, 153; opposes capital punishment, 24-25, 46; opposed limiting offices in woman's temperance society to women, 17; paper is the outstand-

ing champion of woman's rights, 16-17; pledges fight for woman suffrage after ratification of Fifteenth Amendment; 34-35; praises North Star Association, 11; presence at woman suffrage conventions resented by Southern suffragists, 40; proud of his support of woman suffrage, 113; relations with his first wife, 21-23; role at anti-capital punishment meeting, 24-25, 46; role at Seneca Falls Convention, 13-14, 73, 177-79; speaks once during Civil War on woman's rights, 26; on special discrimination against slave women, 19, 76; speech before New England Woman Suffrage Association, 116-24; speech before Woman Suffrage Association, 109-16; splits with William Lloyd Garrison, 19-22, 147, 153, 154, 155; supports Elizabeth Cady Stanton's resolution for woman suffrage, 13-14; supports woman suffrage, 90-92; tells women why they must fight for their rights, 59; temperance reformer, 17-18; tribute to anti-slavery women, 11, 105-06, 132-33, 156-67; tribute to black women, 51-53; tribute to Lucy Stone, 164-67; tributes to by women, 41-42; tributes to disturb Southern suffragists, 43; turning point in life, 8; on women suffrage on different basis from Negro suffrage, 77-78; works for suffrage for New York women, 29

Douglass, Frederick, Jr., 22
Douglass, Helen Pitts, 41, 154, 181